SHIFT
Three Big Moves for the 21st Century Church

Mark E. Tidsworth

What others are saying about *SHIFT: Three Big Moves for the 21st Century Church*

"In *Shift: Three Big Moves For The 21st Century Church*, Mark Tidsworth provides new language for pastors and congregations seeking to understand the seismic cultural transitions happening around us and our instinctive responses to them. Rather than living in fear or apathy these shifts invite us into an invigorating new adventure of faith in Jesus and the church. As a pastor, I am grateful for writers like Mark guiding us into a deeper engagement with the Bible, our faith, and Postmodern American."

Rev. Dr. Eric Spivey, Pastor
First Baptist Church, Cornelia, GA

"Mark has a pilgrim's desire, a pastor's heart and a therapist's insight. Through *Shift: Three Big Moves For The 21st Century Church*, the reader gets a rare look at what is learned through engagement with hundreds of leaders over the years. Mark helps all of us make sense of what we are seeing in congregations and culture. Most importantly, he moves quickly from assessment to offering solid clues about how to respond in ways that are deeply faithful to Christian tradition."

Rev. Dr. Dave Odom, Executive Director
Leadership Education at Duke Divinity

"In his book *Shift: Three Big Moves For The 21st Century Church*, Mark Tidsworth describes the struggle to move away from the status quo of Modernity to a new paradigm of a "disciple developing missional church that practices sacred partnering." While recognizing the reality that the final image of Postmodern Christendom is still unfolding, he offers concrete suggestions for exploration and experimentation intended to lead a church into a new way of being church. Furthermore, Tidsworth does not promise increased average Sunday attendance or more generous stewardship. Rather, he suggests that churches who follow his recommendations will experience satisfaction with their corporate walk with Christ, saying, "We are doing something meaningful here." And in the meantime those involved will experience a deeper relationship with Christ and one another. I recommend this book for pastors and lay leaders who are dissatisfied with church-as-we-have-always-done-it and are seeking ideas for deepening relationships with Christ and one another in community."

Rev. Mike Flanagan, Rector
Holy Cross Episcopal Church, Simpsonville, SC

"This is the most helpful book I have read on the current reality of the church. As a pastor who is dealing with these issues, I feel that Tidsworth was speaking to my questions and concerns. The book not only states the current reality, but offers helpful strategies based on a correct assessment of the church. The strategies will, I believe, enable local churches to experience the renewal they so desperately desire."

Rev. Dr. Mike Guffee, Senior Pastor
Shandon United Methodist Church, Columbia, SC

"You will want Mark Tidsworth to come lead your team in the Shift Learning Experience after you read *Shift: Three Big Moves for the 21st Century*. If you see church-as-we-have-known-it fading away and wonder what you can do to help chart a course for fresh expressions of Christianity going forward, Shift is the book for you. With clarity and understanding, Tidsworth accomplishes the rare feat of bridging the gap between the thirty-thousand-foot metanarrative and the useful here's-what-you-can-do-about-it. Insightful yet practical, Shift is a valuable resource for ministers and church leadership teams who want to take a proactive approach to thinking and planning for the future."

Rev. Dr. Rhonda Abbott Blevins Executive Coordinator
Kentucky Baptist Fellowship

"Finally, a book that gives voice to the vague feelings of uneasiness we have had for a long time. More than identifying the current reality, Mark Tidsworth also offers guidance for how to think and act our way toward partnering more fully with what God is doing in our changing world. The three main Paradigm Shifts outlined in this book will confirm what you are noticing and provide a helpful and hope filled way toward a renewed vision for how to live our faith and be the church in today's world."

Rev. Tisha Brown
Associate Conference Minister for Leadership Development
Wisconsin Conference, UCC

"As a church planter I believe this book will be helpful to anyone starting a new church. And it will also be of value to the church that wants to reach people in our times."

-Mark's Dad, Rev. Floyd Tidsworth
Church Planter and Strategist, semi-retired

"Everyone who loves and leads the church has felt the cultural ground shifting beneath our feet. Mark Tidsworth, out of his illuminating research into our new cultural and religious realities, and his personal insights gained in the daily ministry of helping churches and ministers understand their present and discover their future, offers us a wake-up call, a reality check, a direction to follow and a much-needed message of hope: the church must change, but it need not die. Shifts will inspire you to let go of old the wineskins of outmoded structures and strategies and take hold of skins that can hold the new wine of church as disciples together on mission."

Dr. Ronald D. Vaughan, Lead Pastor
St. Andrews Baptist Church, Columbia, SC

"For over a decade Mark has been a mentor, helping me connect with the changing cultural reality in which we do ministry. *Shift: Three Big Moves For The 21st Century Church* is an invitation to acknowledge these changes and to let the Holy Spirit guide our congregations in imagining and practicing ministry in new ways. As you read you will find yourself responding with a "YES!" over and over again."

Rev. Wayne Horne, Lead Pastor
Union United Methodist Church, Irmo, SC

"A burst of fresh air to fill the sails of the Church of Jesus Christ... Mark provides a window through which to see the realities of our times, and then presents a guide, more framework than road map, to follow. As a lead pastor, I appreciate Mark giving us the language to navigate these Postmodern waters in order to be a part of God's mission in this world."

Rev. Laura Smith Conrad, Lead Pastor
Fort Hill Presbyterian Church, Clemson, SC

"Anxiety is high in congregations feeling the pressure to change in order to engage Postmodern adults. We know we need to change but into what? And how do we do it? Mark Tidsworth's "Shift" shines as a ray of hope and a directional beacon for congregations seeking a path to 21st century ministry. Mark clearly describes the cultural movements that cause the tension between inherited church forms and the need for new expressions within the community of faith. But much more than another description of the "problem with church," he prescribes three "shifts" that will engage renewed faith: from membership to discipleship identity, from attractional to missional church, from consumer church to sacred partnering. Mark moves us from understanding the anxious moments of change to specific practices that facilitate the "shifts" necessary for thriving ministry. Mark Tidsworth's *"Shift: Three Big Moves for the 21st Century Church"* should be a go-to guide for congregations as they plan their future."

Rev. Dr. Jay Keive, Coordinator
Cooperative Baptist Fellowship of South Carolina

"Most Christians and congregations will agree that church does not feel like it did years ago. Mark Tidsworth advances disciple movement in *Shift: Three Big Moves For The 21st Century Church*, leading Jesus followers from the impulse of being consumed by culture in God's church to how the church can join God's mission to love and save the world. You will recognize yourself and your congregation in these perceptive and "how to" pages leading you to see your ministry through new and missional lenses."

Rev. Lane D. Bembenek, Lead Pastor
Joy Lutheran Church (ELCA) Spartanburg, SC

What does it take for members of the church to be the church in the world? Join Mark Tidsworth on an instructive journey that calls for the development of mature discipleship capable of motivating the people of God into action. *Shift: Three Big Moves for the 21st Century* is an essential resource for anyone who seeks to lead a mission-minded congregation or any community of faith.

Rev. Dorothy "d'Rue" Massey Hazel, Canon for Congregational Development and Administration, Deacon in the Diocese of Upper South Carolina , Episcopal Diocese of Upper South Carolina

"I'm playing catch up with e-mail and landed on this one, where I decided to peruse the first part of your manuscript before moving on quickly. Many more minutes later than I intended, I'm forcing myself to stop reading, so I can get back to catching up. I'm hooked and can't wait to find time to continue reading."

Mark's Big Sister, Dr. Constance Campbell, W. E. Carter
Distinguished Chair in Business Leadership, and
Professor of Management
Georgia Southern University, Statesboro, GA

"In these days of discontinuous change, Shift gives us some clear and exciting direction for our journey into the future God has for the church. Shift challenges us not to revert to our defaults of the past, but to embrace the truth that it is God's mission that has a church rather than a church that has a mission."

Rev. Dr. T. Mark Verdery
General Presbyter/Stated Clerk
Providence Presbytery, Rock Hill, SC

"Tidsworth's book should be required reading for anyone in the pew or the pulpit. He is bold enough to name the 'elephant in the room' but he doesn't just name it. He offers practical wisdom on how to tackle it, one bite at a time."

Rev. Dr. Cathy Jamieson-Ogg
Columbia District Superintendent
South Carolina Conference, United Methodist Church

"The first time I changed gears in my used-but-new-to-me 1985 Honda Civic five-speed, it was a tragedy of comedic proportions: a jumping car, startled bystanders, and a rattled driver. It was a great life lesson. Learning to 'shift' takes practice, perseverance and tenacity – but the end result is well worth it. As Mark

Tidsworth skillfully leads us through what it means for communities of faith to shift their focus from creating 'good members' to molding 'ministers of reconciliation,' you will find yourself at many points feeling jumpy, startled and rattled – but you will also hear a still, small Voice whispering: 'this is a way that leads to life; walk ye in it.'"

Rev. Bob Bauman, Harbor District Superintendent,
North Carolina Conferernce, United Methodist Church

"Although many congregations have tried to avoid engaging with or understanding the changing landscape that has been facing the Church for many years, we can hide no longer. For many different reasons, the Church is no longer seen as a vital point of relationship or engagement for many communities. Through personal experience and relevant stories, the author clearly explains the many obstacles faced by the Church and gives well thought out options for the Church to reengage with its members and communities. Shift is a reasonable and measured assessment of the changing landscape that the Church has been facing for many years, as well as an intuitive guide to be followed by congregations who want to move from a place of frustration to a place of fulfillment. As the pastor of a congregation that has experienced many of the things that the author mentions, I will take heed to his words of wisdom and encourage our congregation to do the same."

Rev. Dr. Terrell Carter, Pastor, Author
Pinnacle Leadership Associate, St. Louis, MO

"I am pleased that I chose to attend the Shift Continuing Education Event. I was pleased that Mark presented the topic in the context of the discussion of the whole post-modern Christian reality in the world. I was pleased that the approach was how to struggle with being "faithful" as a mission-driven disciple of Jesus Christ, as opposed to the standard church leadership presentation of how to be "successful" with (numbers & dollars) if you do it like Pastor John Doe at XYZ Mega Church."

Rev. Edward Ebersole
Mandarin Lutheran Church, ELCA, Florida

"Shift was so very helpful for me - affirming trends and movements I've sensed were afoot, and taking me further with new language, new insights, and supporting data."

The Rev. Karen S. Hawkins
Interim Pastor, St. Johannes Lutheran Church
Charleston, SC

"The Shift Learning Experience has helped give me a language to express the feelings of change and loss that is being experienced in my congregation today and also gave me a template to help guide me in this continuing journey. An added benefit was meeting fellow pilgrims who are sharing this same journey."

Rev. Rebecca Shirley
Platt Springs United Methodist Church
West Columbia, SC

CONTENTS

PREFACE

Three Questions Saved My (Spiritual) Life

I was nearly done, making me almost a Done (previously very
active church leaders who quit church in frustration). Between
2005-2006, our family experienced the perfect storm of trying
circumstances. Chronic illness, extended family changes, my
workplace shifting for the worse, the new church we were in
struggling to make it...plus, I was doing conflict management
consulting with several churches at once – an activity designed to
suck the soul right out of a person. All of this nearly turned me
into one of the Dones, a person who believed I could no longer
find God in the church-as-I-have-known-it.

I was afraid during that year and a half back in 2005-6, I would
have to find a new ministry. Finding God in the institutional
church felt like a hide and seek game. "God, show yourself...
surely you are in here somewhere."

A strange thing happened as I headed out the church door. Three
questions saved my (spiritual) life. They presented themselves
through reading, conversations, reflection, and I'm not sure from
where else. Regardless from where they came, I am so thankful

for them. Now I can't stop pursuing, investigating, exploring, and following when it comes to God's movement in this world.

What does it mean to be a disciple of Jesus Christ?

No really, what does it mean? Back then I thought I knew the answers and... I was wrong. I wasn't completely wrong; but my answers were insufficient for living in the Way of Jesus in this Postmodern context. If you think you know the answers before deeply exploring the scriptures and engaging others involved in this quest, then you are assuming way too much (and we know what that makes of us).

What does it mean, now, in this Postmodern context, to follow Jesus Christ? When we orient our lives around Jesus, how do our lives take shape? When we explore the Way of Jesus as described in the gospels, what do we find – and then how do we live that? When Jesus asked us to pray that God's kingdom would come here on earth as it is in heaven, did he actually intend for the kingdom to do so? And all those sayings in the Sermon on the Mount; the ones about loving enemies...was he serious? And forgiveness...even when the other doesn't admit he/she is wrong or is not sorry at all? How in the world do you expect me to do this? That would take power and strength beyond what's natural. And then what about sharing my material resources with others who don't have a coat (basic necessities)? Did Jesus know this would conflict with my American-shaped cultural standards? Just what does it mean to live in the robust Way of Jesus Christ? This question drew me in, like a moth whirring around the back porch light on a cool summer evening. Trying to answer honestly, with authenticity, and then ordering life around the answers...this is a life-long project worth pursuing.

What does it mean to be a gathered community of disciples?

When these Christ followers get together, what do they do? How do they spend their time? In what ways do they help one another answer the previous question? In what ways do they help each other when they fail? What can they do for one another when one is overwhelmed by the quest, cringing in the corner with fear? Do they speak the truth to one another in love, challenging each other when they grow arrogant or complacent? What do they encourage each other to do with their money? And how does the gospel influence how they use their collective money? Does being church the way they are currently church to each other reflect the spirit and example of Jesus? Would Jesus willingly lay down his life so that this way of being church could continue? When I visualize joining with other Christ-followers to be Christian community to one another my heart leaps and my spiritual passion burns hot.

What does it mean to be a gathered community of disciples who join God on mission in the world?

When these gathered disciples decide to do something, how do they decide? How much do they believe the teachings of Jesus are meant for transforming this world? With whom do they partner, or not partner, as they engage other organizations? Do they believe they have the corner on God and are bringing God to their community, or do they believe God is already in their community doing something? How do they know when they are living out their collective calling? Is there room in their view of the world for personal sacrifice in service of God's mission?

When I started asking these questions, it became clear I had a long way to go toward answering them. My way of life was clearly more shaped by my culture than my faith. Now I'm on the road, moving toward answers. Now I'm always looking for partners who will ask the questions and try to live the answers with me. These questions have launched me into a quest which will take an invigorated, robust, faith-based life to answer. They saved my (spiritual) life, breathing life into my worn-out lifeless faith.

But then came another dilemma....
Where to find a Christian faith community gathered around these questions.

INTRODUCTION

With some distance and objectivity, we can see that church-as-we-have-known-it is over. Even in the most culturally traditional and isolated places in this country, the culture which collaborated with Christian churches during the Modern Era is shifting. Many are fleeing their traditional denominationally-based churches for

1. The largest churches of their denomination. In their community this may be "First Church" or "The Cathedral." These faith communities still have the resources to sustain church-as-we-have-known-it. Often they will collect church refugees from mid-size or small churches who cannot sustain their way of being church. These refuges find a familiar church model in these larger regional faith communities. But this is a short-term proposition, since their recruits are Christians fleeing from smaller churches or those in crisis. This stream of recruits to a now older expression of Christianity grows ever smaller as people age, or just walk away.
2. Mega-churches. Many mega-churches are growing, along with their satellite locations, turning into a Christian franchise movement. We applaud this. Yet, we also

observe plenty of people who used to go to a big box church. They just couldn't sustain the necessary hype required to really participate in the high energy worship. They came to see it as one big enthusiastic show for Jesus each Sunday, without much substance. Others would never go through mega-church doors in the first place due to their suspicion of this kind of Christian expression. Some part of our population does and will continue to resonate with this expression of the Christian faith...but it's a small percentage of our population.

Something's changed.
This is the feeling, the experience, the awareness just under the surface in so many churches in North America now. People sense it, experience it, are aware of it...without ways to make sense of their experience.

Questions.
That's what many sincere Christ-following people are left with at this point in history.
   -Is the good news still good news?
   -Does this world need Jesus Christ as much as it did before?
   -What's happening in the Church?
   -Is the Church still a viable organism in the 21st century?
   -What are we doing wrong?
   -Why aren't we getting the results we used to get with the same high quality ministry activities?
   -What's going on here?
   -Is there hope for the Christian church in our society now?

Anyone who is paying attention in Christian churches is clear that the ground beneath our feet is shifting. Things are not as they once were. Simultaneously, many in Christian churches have not found ways to understand their experience, leaving them to wonder what's happening.

Shifts.

Each era in history has its themes.

In these Postmodern times in which the North American Church finds itself, the ground beneath its feet is shifting. Sometimes we experience these as seismic shifts, with tectonic plates raising up new landscapes before us. We encounter new mountains to climb with wonderful vistas to discover. Other times the land before us drops suddenly and we stumble down into sinkholes, experiencing loss of the familiar and known. Either way, the context of the Christian Church as we have known it is radically shifting. Church-as-we-have-known-it is coming to an end. I do not mean that the Christian Church is ending. I believe great days are ahead for the Christian movement in God's world. Yet, I also clearly believe that the way we have been church during the Modern Era is drawing to a close.

Before we examine the context further, reminding ourselves of the purpose of this Christian movement will give us clarity of purpose and direction. When it comes to Scripture, there are many places where we gain clarity on the purpose of God's Church. The basic calling of God's people seems to be laser focused in the New Commandment and the Great Commission.

The New Commandment

> *"I give you a new commandment, that you love one another. Just as I have loved you, you also should love one another. By this everyone will know that you are my*

7

disciples, if you have love for one another."

John 13:34-35, NRSV

Have you noticed how Jesus in the gospels did not emphasize commandments? Yes, he does answer questions about which commandments of old are the greatest (See Matthew 22 and Mark 12). Often though, Jesus described another way of living, rich with metaphors and analogies, while his teachings are light on commandments. That is why the choice of the phrase "new commandment" in John 13 is so striking. The context of this statement is the farewell discourse of Jesus, preparing the disciples for his crucifixion and ascension. These sayings are like the last opportunity Jesus has to give his best instructions before parting with his closest disciples. Afterwards we easily imagine the disciples remembering this commandment, given the significant way it was delivered. It's like Jesus was saying, "When you are caught up in the swirl and stress of life, when you are not sure what to do next, when you lose your way, then remember this commandment – love each other." This is the bottom line for Christ-followers. When we are not sure what to do, this is the place to return for guidance. Love one another. When we do this, we most resemble our Lord. When we forget or ignore this commandment, we lose our way. Above all else, we are called and commissioned to love one another.

The Great Commission

> *And Jesus came and said to them, "All authority in heaven and on earth has been given to me. Go therefore and make disciples of all nations, baptizing them in the name of the Father and of the Son and of the Holy Spirit, and teaching them to obey everything that I have commanded you. And remember, I am with you always,*

to the end of the age."

Matthew 28:18-20, NRSV

We tend to call this passage The Great Commission. Growing up in my denomination, this passage was nearly always interpreted as a call to evangelism. It was something we do to those who are out there in the world; a call to convert the masses to the Christian faith. Though the evangelistic call is certainly here, my understanding of this call has shifted. Now, I believe I am one of those who needs to become a disciple of Jesus Christ. As I endeavor to follow Jesus, I realize I am a disciple while also not yet a disciple. Christ has claimed me, yet there are parts of myself which are not yet converted. Becoming a disciple is a life-long journey of formation. Yes it has beginnings, yet it is never complete, this side of heaven. I am a disciple of Jesus Christ, I am becoming a disciple of Jesus Christ, and I shall be a disciple of Jesus Christ. Making disciples includes me. I am a part of the disciple-making movement of God in the world. So, our calling is to make disciples of ourselves and others until the end of all things.

If this is the calling of the Christian Church (New Commandment and Great Commission), then one has to wonder if this calling remains relevant. Does the world need more love? Does the world need people who look through the lens of love when they make decisions or when they form attitudes about others? Does the world need groups of people (churches) who aspire to loving one another as their primary purpose? Does the world need Jesus Christ; a caring God who calls humanity to live this life of love? Do the teachings of Jesus provide another way to live which is hopeful and life-giving? Perhaps this good news of the gospel is needed at the same level in every historical era, but it seems like

9

this gospel is needed more now than ever. This is the opportune time for loving disciple-developing missional churches to rise up and be who they are called to be. Now is the time to shift.

The flow of this book follows a rhythm from here onward. These three big moves for the 21st century church are organized into sections. Each section describes the decline of the Modern Era Church's relationship to this move followed by the rise of this newer movement in the Postmodern Era Church. Suggestions for making the shift follow, giving clues toward pursuing being church in a new way. Before we start shifting though, we need an understanding of why these shifts are necessary. Part One describes the context wherein North American faith communities find themselves.

PART ONE
CONTEXTING

This was the best class ever. Why isn't everyone at this college registering for this class, trying to get in so they can soak up these insights? That was my thought process after finding myself in a Social Psychology Class in 1984. The professor described so many fascinating social science experiments which surfaced insights into how culture and society shape human perspective. The text told these stories too, through the lens of experiment after experiment. We learned stories of teachers who expected students to be bright or dull, influencing the student's performance due to the teacher's expectations. We learned about groups of otherwise caring people ignoring pleas for help when group norms constrained their actions. We discovered that self-disclosure (sharing one's stuff) by one person establishes a cultural norm of openness, eliciting self-disclosure by others in one's group. The bottom line of this Social Psychology Class was that we homo sapiens see what we are conditioned to see, experiencing our world as our culture conditions us to experience our world.

Culture is like the river in which we swim. It's very similar to time

– we are so immersed in time that we cannot imagine life without its passage. Culture functions this way too. The norms, perspectives, pressures, principles, expectations, and mores of our time contribute to culture's formation. Technology, economics, and religion are all influences on culture, while also being shaped by culture. Culture is the context for the living of our days.

Given this, we accept that the Church shapes culture, while being shaped by culture. Looking back at the Church during any historical time period, we recognize culture as a major shaping influence on how we are church. Musical styles, worship times, stance toward technology in worship, modes of Christian formation, governance....all these, along with everything else we do, are symbiotically connected to the culture of the times.

Now it is fascinating to explore this cultural river in which we Postmodern Christ-followers swim.
It turns out, that culture is not everything, yet culture is related to everything.

Culture is the river in which we swim.

CHAPTER ONE
THE RIVER IN WHICH WE SWIM

So if something has changed, and it is not less of a need for the gospel, then what is the change about? Fortunately many bright authors, researchers, ministers, and social scientists are describing the move in our culture from Modernity to Postmodernity. The worldview which has been in place in Europe and North America the last 500 years or so has shifted. We are not far enough into this new era to have developed understandings or categories for what's happening, so we simply call this time "Postmodernity." We know things are not like they were before, yet they are not clear enough to describe what will take place in the present and future. The formation of this era is not clear, the themes have not settled into paradigms or models as of yet.

Phyllis Tickle is great help for us in understanding the contextual changes for Church since the year 2000. She cleverly uses the metaphor of a rummage sale, describing what's happening in her book *The Great Emergence* (2008).[1] About every 500 years, the Church clears out its attic, holding a rummage sale. The sign out front reads, "Everything must go." Tickle traces these major shifts in the life of the Church including:

- 30-70AD – Birth of the church – 70-130: decline of Judaism
- 590AD (or so) – Fall of the Roman Empire and Beginning of the Dark Ages
- 1054AD – The Great Schism – Church divided between East and West
- 1517 (or so) – The Great Reformation and Beginning of The Modern Period
- 2000 + - Postmodern Period

The result of this Rummage Sale experience is that we are living in a new era. Again we are unsure of what to call it, simply knowing it is "Post" what was before. Though we don't yet have models or paradigms, we do have insights into the nature of the Postmodern Movement.

Postmodern people do not endorse any one pervasive worldview, yet believe there are a diversity of perspectives for understanding the world. This revolving planet we inhabit is so much smaller than it used to be. The internet, along with hundreds of other technological advances, brings the world to my fingertips. We live with far more awareness about world events as they occur, along with exposure to varied people groups far outside the lines of our own subcultures. These advances force us to think more broadly. Religiously, this means that the diversity we experience is not simply the myriad of Christian denominations. Now we are in touch with people from most of the world's religions, along with those who do not engage organized faith systems at all. All of this results in a diversity of perspective when it comes to understanding the world, understanding humankind, and our place in the universe. Earlier in America's history, there was less diversity, with more of a shared world view. Now people see the world through a broad array of lenses.

Postmodern people believe this universe is more complex and expansive than we realized. Those of us indoctrinated with the Modern worldview learned that the scientific method, properly applied, was a reliable process for discovering truth. Facts, logic, rational thought led to an accurate understanding of reality, along with tools for discovery of what is yet unknown. As it turns out, this universe is more complex than we realized, preventing the scientific method, rational approaches, and logical thought from discovering all truth. Now scientists, those previously dogmatic about the scientific method, are pushing the envelope, promoting the idea that other ways of knowing can be real and effective. No longer is there one (or just a few) worldview, nor is there one way of knowing and describing reality.

Postmodern people believe that the diversity in the world makes subjective experience and context far more important when it comes to identifying truth, reality, and relevance. Since there is such diversity, establishing truths that persist across cultures is difficult. Many Postmodern people are going local. What makes sense in your local context? What's the truth of this community? What's real and lasting as you interpret life; you being a community of faith or an individual? The local context drives Postmodern understandings of what's real and genuine. At the same time, one's experience in life is also considered a very reliable guide for direction. An emphasis on one's individual journey, and the lessons learned, is rising as a way to set direction for life.

Postmodern people are far more open to spirituality, especially in terms of mystery and experience, than those of the Modern Era. Since logic, rationality, and cognition cannot explain all of experience, then the place of spirituality is growing. Postmodern people believe there are ways of knowing beyond what our cognitive abilities can know (non-rational and non-objective). This perspective diminishes the view of universal objective truths, and raises the interest in discovering truth through spiritual and subjective experiences. Scientists of the Modern Era may have dismissed spirituality due to its resistance to definition through the scientific method. Now many scientists are leaders calling for the inclusion of spirituality in the pursuit of understanding the universe. As you might think, spirituality and religion are not synonymous. Yet, Postmodern people see spiritual mystery as valid and even necessary to a well-lived life.

Postmodern people increasingly distrust institutions. When culture and social norms begin breaking-down, the organizations built upon that culture and its norms also experience disruption. The shift to the Postmodern era is raising questions about everything in society. Institutions and organizations, seen as icons of a certain era, are receiving much criticism as the shift becomes more clear. We have to admit, some of the criticism and suspicion is well-placed, given the excesses (financial, moral, social, breach of trust, etc.) of leaders in the Modern Era. These contribute to the suspicion and distrust already rising in the Postmodern Era.

Postmodern people increasingly choose to trust others based on genuineness and authenticity. Positional authority existed in the Modern Era. Simply because one was in a position of authority or influence, we believed this person deserved respect and generous levels of trust. Now, positional authority does not mean much (see the paragraph above). Now more than ever, trust must be earned. Genuineness, one's authenticity, is a major factor in whether we will trust persons in positions of influence. Skills and

(don't care what you know until they know that you care)

position alone will not elicit respect. Now leaders and authority figures must have depth of personhood to back up their skill set. Authenticity, being a real person first before filling a role, is necessary for Postmodern persons to trust one's influence.

These shifts begin making sense of congregational experience. Many churches know that something has changed without a way for understanding what's happening. Recognizing the perspectives of Postmodern people helps pull back the cloak over our reality.

Though understanding Postmodern perspectives is helpful, we are left with a major dilemma as churches trying to live our faith. Frequently we observe clergy, lay leaders, and congregations struggling with their reality, feeling very stretched. They have one foot solidly planted in the Modern Era institutional church-as-we-have-known-it. This means they own property which comes with maintenance needs and costs, they employ people with salaries and taxes to pay, and they are organizations which need regular attention to keep running. They are organizations with constitutions and by-laws. Many have a franchise-like relationship with their denomination...receiving policies, procedures, and practices from headquarters. These churches are clearly designed with the Modern Era organizational model in play.

At the very same time, their other foot feels like it's planted on another planet. Their people are living in the Postmodern world. The businesses, corporations, and educational institutions around them are morphing into something different. People in their communities have changed their perspectives. They are dropping the layers of their Modern Era worldview daily, while replacing them with Postmodern perspectives. Naturally, these people bring their emerging Postmodern perspectives to church with them, expecting church to mirror their emerging Postmodern worldview.

So churches and their leaders are doing the Modern to Postmodern Stretch. Here is how we hear them describing their dilemma.

"We are leading Modern Era institutions while living in this Postmodern context."

Leaders still must tend to the needs of our Modern Era constructed organizations (churches) while also adapting to the new realities in which we are swimming in this Postmodern Era. We are in the transition time between the two, so our straddle posture is real.

Every church is formed in a context, with certain cultural norms contributing to its formation. The majority of churches in North American are clearly imprinted with the cultural norms of the Modern Era. The Builder Generation, with their tremendous energy for building a newer, better society after World War II, left a lasting imprint on the way congregations are structured and formed. Many people can barely even think of church without assuming the way we do church is THE way to be church. Integrating the cultural norms and social customs of one's day into the formation of the church is a natural process. The early church certainly was formed in a similar manner. So there is nothing inherently wrong or evil in this reality. This is how organizations of all kinds are formed.

The dilemma inherent within this reality is that when culture and society radically change, the institutions which were formed with the previous worldview, find themselves in a strange new land. They continue to operate with the assumptions of a previous era, while living in the current era. This puts them in the transition zone; a state of being in-between.

Perhaps a practical example will help. My father served as a denominational minister throughout much of his ministry. He was fascinated with the kinds of contexts wherein churches flourished. I remember one conversation from the early 1980s. He was describing new and established churches which are in population centers in the Southeastern United States. "If a church can do two or three things really well, then it will grow (numerically)." In this statement he was describing the reality for churches who applied themselves in effective ways during the Modern Era; or the age of Christendom. At that time, when there still was a basic Christian culture in parts of the United States, a church with several quality initiatives, ministries, or programs could gather significant numbers of people.

I reflected on this conversation with my father as I listened to a lead pastor describing the dilemmas in her congregation. The church wherein she served is a healthy church, with about 300 in worship, between two services. This pastor works far too much, applying herself to her calling with vigor and enthusiasm. The laity in this congregation are dedicated and committed. The church is staffed with excellence. Their facilities are up to date and their programming is good. They clarified their vision through a discernment process and are focused, advancing major goals. Still, they are not numerically growing like they expect to grow. I found myself saying to this pastor, "If you were doing the same thing, if this church was doing the same thing in your community during the 1970s, then you would see about 1000 people in worship each weekend." During the Modern Era, this church, doing what it is doing now, would have involved so many people. Now, things have changed. The "return on investment" of Modern Era shaped church initiatives is far lower in this Postmodern Culture.

These examples illustrate the possibility that it may not be the quality or level of effort holding the church back - it may be the church's paradigm. We are leading Modern Era institutions while living in the Postmodern Era. The return on investment so to speak, is not what it was. When we observe the results of our efforts at being and doing church declining, one explanation may be that we are working from a paradigm which no longer connects with our culture. This is not about being unfaithful to the gospel by adopting the moral values of a secular culture. This is about recognizing the ways people relate, communicate, and engage the world are different than before.

All of this raises significant questions for the Christian Church. When we begin listing the questions, notice how they are questions driven by Modern Era perspectives:

- What does regular and consistent church attendance look like now?
- How can we get people to volunteer more?
- How can we reach the younger people in our community?
- What worship style do we need in order to grow as a church?
- Why won't people give more to our unified church budget?

We could list many more. We hear these questions frequently in our leadership coaching and church consulting from concerned leaders. These kinds of questions are those which churches still operating from the Modern worldview ask and pursue. They indicate a desire to restore, renew, and reinvigorate church-as-we-have-known-it. Questions are powerful influences, determining what we become. These questions are indicative of congregations who have not yet shifted.

For better or worse, the Modern Era with its cultural norms is over, or at least nearly over. Fewer churches are likely to return to being church in the manner they used to be. Yes, there are exceptions. There are cultural enclaves where enough is the same to sustain Modern Era churches. These are the temporary exception, rather than the rule.

This takes me back to a conversation during my seminary training in evangelism class. Dr. Lewis Drummond, a great revival preacher, described the changing world around us well. "You have a different challenge before you as newer ministers than do I. I'm an old preacher who can still be invited to do revivals in small towns until the day I die. But you, you know revival services are aging-out. You will have to discover how to engage your culture with the gospel in ways very different than for my generation." This insightful professor described the challenge for every generation: how to be church and live the gospel faithfully, while also in culturally relevant ways.

If the questions we ask form us, what are the questions of churches who are letting go of their Modern Era roots and moving into the 21st century? These churches are the ones driven to the roots or foundations of their faith. They are diving deep into the waters of mission, purpose, and calling. They find themselves in contexts similar to the early church, causing them to grow clear on what it's all about anyway.

- What does it mean to be a disciple of Jesus Christ now?
- How seriously are we willing to engage Jesus' teachings?
- How much are we caught up in living in the Way of Jesus?
- When Jesus-followers band together in a group, what do they do?
- What's the nature of this Christian community called the Church?
- If we wanted to form a group which helps its members to live out the teachings of Jesus, what would we do?
- What kind of sacred partnerships do we need in this faith community to support/challenge us to live as disciples?
- How would we form ourselves as a faith community if we intended to seriously answer the questions above?

These questions are far more formational, involving deep change. When eras shift, everything comes loose. This is a time for asking the primal questions. Only this kind of exploration will lead us to join with God's unfolding story in this world.

CHAPTER TWO
WHEN THE CURRENT CHANGES DIRECTION

Coaching clergy and consulting churches provides the
opportunity for observing the reactions of churches to our
shifting context. The variety of reactions is fascinating. As
you read through the following, consider where your
congregation may be in its journey. Some of the following
reactions are more adaptive than others, as you will notice.
I offer these descriptions with no judgment. Change is
difficult and resistance is inevitable. We must grow
sufficiently convinced that what we are doing is not
advancing the mission before we will change. Perhaps these
are points on the developmental response continuum when
we encounter unexpected change, when currents change
direction. Clergy, church staff, lay persons, and entire
congregations find themselves somewhere on this response
continuum.

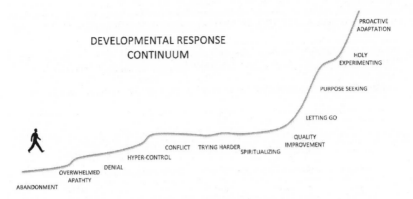

DEVELOPMENTAL RESPONSE
CONTINUUM

PROACTIVE
ADAPTATION

HOLY
EXPERIMENTING

PURPOSE SEEKING

LETTING GO

QUALITY
IMPROVEMENT

CONFLICT   TRYING HARDER
SPIRITUALIZING

HYPER-CONTROL

DENIAL

OVERWHELMED
APATHTY

ABANDONMENT

Abandonment

Early on, no one notices abandonment happening. One family leaves because they want more programming for their children. Another couple leaves because they would like to be in a church with people their own age. Another simply stops participating, dropping out of the Christian Church altogether. It takes several leavings before church leaders recognize the abandonment pattern. Few people are angry or irritated with this church; not leaving because of overt conflict. Instead, due to ongoing low-level disappointment, boredom, and hopelessness, they just drift away. The engagement factor in this congregation dips so low that people find themselves adrift, feeling like it wouldn't matter if they did leave the church. Eventually they do.

Statistics in the United States confirm this. The numbers of people who participate in a Christian church are shrinking, partly because those involved are walking away. They find themselves believing something is missing, the church has grown irrelevant, or they are embarrassed about what the church is saying to its world. Irrelevance of the church, along with disengagement from what's really happening in the world, combine to form a context from which people disengage. Working the Modern Era paradigm of church with Postmodern disciples leaves these disciples high and dry. Eventually they walk away.

How do we know if our congregation is experiencing abandonment? This reaction is very easy to identify. Simply look at participation levels. Is this church numerically shrinking? If so, one explanation may be that it is still living like it's 1965, 1975, or even 1995. What's the eventual outcome? Well, folk wisdom in ministerial circles used to say, "A church is a hard thing to kill." I know clergy who work as parachurch ministers (chaplains, consultants, therapists, etc.) full time and then pastor very small congregations as well. Some of these churches are robust small ministries. Many others are trying to hang on with dignity until the doors close. Some of these congregations have experienced major contextual changes which contributed to their demise, largely external factors. Many more (the majority) made unconscious or conscious choices along the way which led to their demise. Every living organism must adapt to its environment to endure. Not all organisms make it.

Overwhelmed Apathy

What happens to an individual when the pace of change is too fast? How do we react when it seems like we are drinking from a fire hose? When stress becomes distress and we grow overwhelmed, what do we do? A frequent response is to enter a period of apathy.

The 1960s saw a series of psychological and social science studies out of which the term "learned helplessness" evolved. Subjects were exposed to a dilemma, then made to feel like they could not take action which would resolve the dilemma. Over time, subjects just quite trying. Even when conditions obviously changed, making it possible for them to resolve the dilemma, subjects resisted lifting a finger. They had learned helplessness; a posture of inaction in the face of challenges.[1]

Some congregations find themselves experiencing learned helplessness. They see the changes happening in their contexts, they learn about the Postmodern Era's arrival, and they despair. When they look at who they are, they believe things will never change in their congregation, never allowing adaptation. Secretly, the disciples in these congregations believe their church won't ultimately make the changes necessary to flourish in this new world. The limitations, dynamics, norms, and culture of their church are too rigid and ingrained for adaptive change to flourish. When this is one's perspective, then one experiences helplessness. "No matter what we do, things here will not change, so we might as well just live with it."

This reaction is similar to abandonment at its core (belief the church is not and will not adapt), yet the outcome is different. This church has lost who it's going to lose. Those remaining are loyal, caring, dedicated disciples who don't see any other options besides riding it out. They are committed to Christ and to God's Church, never considering walking away. Yet, they see themselves as living on a dead end street – one which has been closed off at both ends. As one might imagine, this perspective (typically unconscious) leads to a lack of energy, momentum, and hope. Apathy becomes the prevailing feeling or ethos of these congregations.

Denial

Why do you participate with a Christian Church? When we are honest, most of us are driven by mixed motivations for being a part of a church. There is the most noble motivation (desire to join with other Christ-followers around God's mission), yet most of carry secondary motivations also. In listening to churches, I hear them expressed in these ways.

> "There are so many changes in my world these days; it's nice to come to the one place where things remain the same."

> "Stress in my life is so high; I'm glad I can come here to a low stress environment."

> "Church (as I have known it) has always been so meaningful to me. Now I want my children (or grandchildren) to have the opportunity for the same kind of experience I had (church done the same way it was done when I was a child)."

We can hear positive intent and healthy motivation mixed in these statements. Yet, they also indicate an expectation that church is the one organism or organization in their world which does not change. This unrealistic expectation is a primary factor driving the denial reaction. When enough individual disciples in a congregation are here, the collective theme in the congregation is denial.

How long can a church keep denial going? You would be amazed at the perseverance of some, partly because one denial effect feels so good to the congregation – turning inward. These congregations turn their energy, resources, and collective emotionality in toward each other, resulting in a temporary strengthening of relational bonds. Some focus this energy into feeling like a persecuted minority ("It's us against the heathen world"), while others simply invest much effort in tending to the needs and wants of one another. Pastors become chaplains, individual care-givers to the disciples in these churches. People feel really loved, largely because the church is self-focused, attentive to every need. Since this all feels so good, denial becomes a hard habit to break.

Hyper-control
We were reflecting on the last year of progress in their church during the annual retreat for the lay leaders. As we went around the room, one gentleman described the church's journey this way. "When things got out of control here, I decided I had been sitting back too much. So I, along with some others who think like me, decided to take back control. We did and now we are on the right track again."

I didn't know how to respond. The story I knew of this church is that a small group had taken control, manipulated the church into a corner, forced the pastor to resign, devastating this faith community in the process. This kind of control led to about half the congregation leaving (church split), and the remaining disciples were emotionally despairing about the future of this church. Fortunately, they were willing to work toward reconciliation and healing, leading to new life. But the hyper-control of this gentleman along with his cohorts led to great pain and suffering, rather than helpful intervention.

One tendency of humankind when we are faced with dynamics beyond our direct control, is to overly invest in controlling what we can. Often this hyper-control is driven by a low-grade anger, just under its surface. We feel like life is doing something to us (removing our control), and that we are losing what's precious to us (our church), so we grow frustrated and irritated. We rush in to take control again.

How do we know when hyper-control is our congregation's response? An effort to improve policies and procedures is a clear sign. Disciples start saying that if we were more organized, more systematic in what we do, with improved job descriptions and better tracking mechanisms...then our church would be fine. The allure of this fantasy is in the beauty of clear policies and procedures printed on nice paper with clear and clean lines of responsibility articulated therein. This can make us feel as if the world is safe again. Everything seems under control because we have a policy or a procedure to tell us what to do in regard to most everything. When the big picture seems out of control, overly-controlling the small picture gives us some level of comfort.

Unfortunately, this hyper-controlling tendency is nearly always maladaptive. It is the exact opposite of what's most needed – yielding to the winds of the Holy Spirit. This is the time to open up, to let go, to follow the Spirit's movement and energy. In fact, many churches continue policies and procedures which are no longer relevant...simply familiar, making them feel safe in a changing world. Clamping down through organizational procedures smothers the Spirit, rather than setting the Spirit free.

Conflict

Does this go without saying? I'm almost embarrassed to describe conflict at this point. Each of the previous reactions can contribute to a rising tension level resulting in church conflict. What drives church conflict and how does it develop?

We are "sense-making" organisms as human beings. Our minds are always working to help us comprehend the world around us. So, when things change for the worse in our church experience, we naturally look for explanations. Without an understanding of the larger dynamics in the world influencing our local context, we assign an explanation to something else. Sometimes this leads to blame, coupled with magic bullet thinking. We diagnose the problem as coming from a single source, along with a fix which is the magic bullet. Here are some magic bullet solution statements, which rest on a foundation of blame.

> "If we just had a more gifted pastor, then our church would be fine."

> "If we spent more time in prayer, then our church would be fine."

"If the music were better or different, then our church would be fine."

"If we would just add a worship service of another style, then our church would be fine."

"If our people would give more generously, then our church could do what it needs to do, and would be fine."

"If our people were more committed (or any other spiritually oriented description), then our church would be fine."

When we think this way, then we seek to eradicate the problem from the church and replace it with the answer. This causes conflict on two levels. First, others don't see the problem the same way, defining it differently. Therefore they do not agree with the suggested fix. Second, the problem is far more expansive than tactical changes can fix, resulting in greater frustration after the fix is applied. Most churches experience some level of conflict when the wheels begin to come off their Modern Era church-as-we-have-known-it paradigm.

Trying Harder

"If we are not getting the results we want, then we are not trying hard enough. We need to apply more effort and engage more fully. Then the results will follow."

There is some truth in this statement, making it alluring. Sometimes we grow lazy as congregations. Sometimes we coast for too long between intense periods of effort.

Sometimes we need to roll up our sleeves and apply ourselves.

This reaction and tactic is helpful under conditions of continuous, incremental change. When the model we are using is still relevant, then working that model more vigorously can be helpful. What happens when the model itself is the problem? This is when we are pounding the proverbial square peg into the round hole. Our answer to the inevitable frustration is to pound harder. The result is increased frustration. Trying harder to force an irrelevant church model to work actually creates greater frustration. Perhaps congregations have to attempt this first, before growing open to new paradigms. Maybe people have to exhaust themselves working an outdated model before they are open to large-scale change.

Spiritualizing
(Is that a word?)
What I mean here is the tendency to see a lack of spirituality, faith, and God-focus as the problem. Perhaps it's unconfessed sin in the church. Perhaps it's a lack of sincere prayer. Perhaps our people are just not committed enough. The lack of spiritual vigor and commitment is seen as the problem.

This reaction too has some truth in it, enough to make it dangerous. At all times, all of us are less than we might be in relationship to God. Who would not want higher levels of faith and a more robust spirituality? Pursuing God and a stronger faith is part of the Christian journey.

Simultaneously, though spiritual renewal always helps, it simply does not address how to be church in the 21st century. The Great Awakenings, which took place periodically throughout America's history, were always accompanied by innovative practices and new methodology. We need increased levels of faith and spirituality in order to have the heart to engage the questions of our day, yet increased faith and spirituality are not the same as engaging the questions of our day. If we are not careful, we find ourselves shaming one another for not being "spiritual" enough. We hear clergy and lay persons alike articulating this perspective regularly. "If our people would just read the Bible more, pray more, grow more committed, etc., then..." The result when we stay with this perspective is that the church feels ashamed of its faith practices, hanging its head in despair. "Not only are we failing as a church, we are shabby Christians too." The downward spiral speeds up when this reaction is practiced.

Quality Improvement

Alan Roxburgh, who writes about the Missional Church Movement, describes this reaction as "shining the apple."[2] If we can improve our quality, then we will regain our glory days as a church. This is the belief behind the quality improvement reaction.

What's fascinating is that a church may find itself with short-term gains when it improves its quality. Christians in other congregations hear about what's happening at this church and they transfer membership. This becomes the "go to" church in its community. They become known as the church with a great youth program, or wonderful choir, or with a new kind of worship service, or with a great new preacher. With time, these churches who improve their quality may find that they are fishing in the Christian pond. They are catching fish, but the fish are swimming over from another aquarium. That pond of fish is limited and small (other Christians), and will be fished out rather quickly. These churches find themselves searching for the next big improvement which will draw others to their church campus. Over time, the next big improvement brings fewer fish. Quality improvement can help any church, yet it does not resolve the dilemmas inherent in moving from the Modern Era to the Postmodern Era.

Letting Go
Now we are moving toward adaptive change. Perhaps the previously mentioned reactions are steps on this adaptive church journey. We have to grow convinced that church-as-we-have-known-it is no longer viable before most of us are willing to relinquish our church paradigm. Perhaps we first have to work the Modern Era church model vigorously, knowing we have laid it all on the line, experiencing lower return on investment, before we willingly let go.

Eventually though, adaptive churches recognize it's time to let go of their way of being church. This step in the journey typically includes quite a mix of emotions. Disciples are relieved they are no longer pressuring themselves to do something they perceive as irrelevant and unhelpful. Disciples also are unsettled, finding themselves in a transition zone, without clarity about how to be church. This is a new experience for many, creating vulnerability when it comes to participating in a faith community. Disciples also experience grief. The way we have been church together includes emotionally charged memories about very meaningful and significant experiences in life. Recognizing those particular practices are going away is sad. Even when we are convinced we must change, the change involves letting go, which brings grief to our experience. Wise congregational leaders recognize this grief, finding ways to help the congregation process and move through the valley of the shadow. Grief management is a key part of the adaptive change process.

Purpose Seeking

Watching congregations move to this point is fascinating. If we could describe their reaction in the previous step of Letting Go with a body movement, it would include a person putting up their hands and backing away from the table. This step, purpose seeking, involves putting our hands down, perhaps on our hips and saying, "Well, what's the purpose of this whole church thing anyway?" When churches start asking this kind of question, we know they are on the way toward a more invigorated expression of their collective faith. In essence they are asking about the mission or purpose of the church. Below this question is another. "Is the mission or purpose of the Church worth all the pain and discomfort we will endure in order to adapt to our current context?"

This is when churches are open to engaging those three life-giving questions. With fresh eyes they read the scriptures. With new openness they engage the teachings of Jesus in the gospels. They experience a kind of conversion or reformation. This conversion is not to faith, but rather to a new freedom in their faith expression. No longer must they do church the way they have done church. Now they re-discover the passion, vigor, and hope of their faith. Reconnecting with the purpose of it all infuses these churches with passionate spirituality. This feels like fresh winds of the Spirit to the weary worn Modern Era spiritual pilgrims.

Holy Experimenting

Later, in Chapter Ten, which describes making the shift toward being a missional church, we will explore holy experimenting in depth. Yet, it's relevant here, because it is a location on this developmental response continuum. After letting go of church-as-we-have-known-it, followed by clarifying what this church-thing is all about anyway (purpose seeking), then faith communities will find themselves experimenting. Some experimenting simply happens because of the movement from one stop on this continuum to the next. Other experiments will be intentionally pursued by the faith community as they engage the movement from one stop to another.

Holy experimenting involves not only giving ourselves permission to experiment, but actively encouraging and pursuing disciple development or missional experimentation. The faith community itself embraces experimentation as a legitimate pathway forward. They affirm experiments, holding up the outcomes as instructive and directional. They believe following the Holy Spirit involves pushing beyond themselves and their comfort zones, discovering new expressions of faith life. These holy experiments then become part of the basis for the next stop on this developmental response continuum.

Proactive Adaptation

Organisms who survive and thrive are those who experiment. They give themselves permission to be different. Sometimes they discover adaptive behaviors by accident. Either way, they are willing to try new ways of being in the world as they find it. Congregations engaged in proactive adaptation have let go of their efforts at returning to church-as-we-have-known-it. They are freed from trying to work a model which provides lower returns on investment. They are actively engaging the world around them, allowing this to shape how they structure church.

During the Shift Learning Experience and Making The Shift Weekends, it's great fun to give participants an opportunity to reflect on where their congregation is in its response to the shifting context. We describe each of the preceding reactions or responses, placing them on an imaginary continuum, inviting disciples to stand where they believe their church is in its developmental process.

Were you to place your congregation on this continuum, where would you stand?

CHAPTER THREE
THE DEMISE OF CHRISTENDOM AND THE RISE OF THE CHRISTIAN MOVEMENT

The demise of Christendom....that sounds so dramatic when said (actually written). Yet, that is exactly what is happening in North America, as Europe experienced before us. The socio-political atmosphere which integrated Christianity into the very fabric of our culture is changed. The popular expression of the church over the last 500 years became normative, resulting in an age of Christendom. The Christian faith became the accepted dominant religion of Western civilization, resulting in many cultural and social advantages for Christianity. This led to the age of Christendom in Europe and North America.

It turns out that the myriad of factors required to allow one form of life to flourish is a fragile state. Small shifts in the environment trigger large-scale changes which disrupt entire ecosystems. This perspective makes sense of what is happing in the North American Church. The age of Christendom, when the factors required for the Church in a certain form to flourish, has shifted. Now the Church, in its typical form, finds itself in an environment less supportive or even antagonistic toward its existence. The typical paradigm for being church is crumbling before our eyes.

What kinds of emotional responses does this awareness evoke from us? There are the more challenging or unpleasant emotions of anxiety, discomfort, fear, and even anger. Many of these accompany those early stages of reacting described in the last chapter. Simultaneously, many of us feel relief when we trace the factors contributing to the demise of Christendom. The unknown is far more intimidating than the known. Knowing what's happening, understanding the cultural shifts behind Christendom's demise, is comforting.

Given this, an excellent way to help your congregation move forward toward a new future is to raise their awareness about what is actually happening. It is time for church leaders to embrace reality as they find it, describing the end of Christendom. When we know God's promises and are in relationship with Almighty God, then describing how our world is changing is far less intimidating. In fact we find great courage for honestly describing things as they are. Many disciples in faith communities are so thankful when we help them understand these shifts. They have been trying to make sense of their church experience for some time. Providing concepts which explain our reality brings great relief. As you can tell from the previous church reaction descriptions, healthier churches move from less adaptive reactions toward proactive response and change.

Where to Now?
This is the question many of us are living now. There are two groups of people who are typically most concerned about change. First, those who are tasked with leading groups through change are highly interested in what leads to effective change. In our

case, this would be clergy, church staff, and lay leaders in congregations. These are the people to whom we look when change is happening and we need guidance on our next steps. Even before guidance for action, we first need frameworks, paradigms, or concepts which help us understand our experiences. We look to leaders when we need leadership. The second group who is very interested in change is those who are most affected by changes. This group would include all those involved in the first group, along with everyone else in the congregation. Anyone who has something to lose or gain as a result of change is interested in the changes. So at this point, does that leave anyone in a congregation out? Change affects us all. We find ourselves in an in-between time, a transition time. The old is passing away as the new is coming along. Here are some phrases we are hearing as people describe the change process in their faith communities:

- Unfolding providence of God
- Evolution of the Church
- Continuing THE Story
- Next iteration of the Church
- Post-Rummage sale days
- Moving from this (old) to that (new)
- Rising up from the ashes
- Moving from death to life
- Letting go and taking hold
- Christian deformation leading to Christian formation
- The Christian Movement

There is good news when we ask ourselves where we are headed. While the rummage sale is on-going, interest in the new items appearing on the shelf is growing. People struggle to find the words to describe new life-giving, faith-based experiences, even in the midst of losing what was (as reflected in the incomplete phrases above). Yet movement is happening in the life of the church. None of these are far enough along to become "models for the 21st century church," while each of these movements indicates the Spirit is alive and well. God's Church continues onward. It may not look like it used to, being dressed quite differently, yet it continues to partner with God for the transformation of the world.

The Christian Movement – Three Signs
Jesus began a movement. Early on this movement was fluid and organic, spreading with a life of its own. There was no strategic planning nor institutional support. A movement focused on following Jesus Christ and living out his teachings organically began and spread.

Now, here at the end of the Modern Era, we find Christianity being transformed again. While its structures and institutions appear to be crumbling, new life is emerging. New impulses are rising from God's people. Though no one knows exactly what the future of our faith looks like, we can see movement happening. In particular, three life giving, encouraging, and very hopeful signs are rising up as we speak. These are shifts from one way of being Christ-followers to another.

Member Identity to Disciple Identity
Attractional Church to Missional Church
Consumer Church to Sacred Partnerships

It turns out that titling a book is harder than one might expect. One run-on, very unwieldy and way too long title I considered was, "Becoming A Disciple Developing Missional Church Who Practices Sacred Partnering." Though not a great book title, this phrase describes what some invigorated faith communities find themselves pursuing. Churches of every size, denomination, and theological perspective are expressing longings to become this kind of church. Some are letting go of their previous paradigms, growing liberated to pursue being disciple developers who join God on mission in the world. When they endeavor to do this, they discover a great need for sacred partnering with other disciples so that they can sustain their forward movement.

At this point, these movements have not resulted in models or paradigms which we can recommend as normative. We are too early in the transition from Modern to Postmodern Era. Yet, we can observe movement happening. These are gaining momentum and taking shape and form. God continues moving over the primeval waters, bringing creativity from chaos.

Moving, transforming, stretching, growing....
We are on the move. God's Church is on the move. Throughout salvation history as described in the Bible, God's people are always on the move. So, though the changes required of us now may be intimidating, they are also exhilarating. There is no way I want to miss out on journeying with God's people the next ten years, discovering a new land together. I want to be there as Christianity moves from an empire-aligned institution to a Spirit-led movement.

See Appendix 3: Sermon – God Is Always On The Move

PART TWO
MEMBER IDENTITY TO DISCIPLE IDENTITY

Introduction
News journalist Tom Brokaw was onto something when he called
them "The Greatest Generation." More accurately, "The Builder
Generation," captures their primary impulse. They built things.
WWII shaped their life experience. The uncertainty of war, along
with the sacrifices it brought to a generation, combined with The
Great Depression experience….all of this galvanized a generation
into a generative people. When the Great Depression was over,
along with the Second World War, a generation stood ready to
build something significant. And build they did, becoming "The
Builder Generation." We now benefit greatly from their focused
effort to build a brave new world, bringing stability and security to
North America. The result was a stable time of growth and
prosperity in this nation. I'm not an expert on this time period, yet
anyone can observe how this played out in the Christian
movement – they built churches.

Not only did they build churches (literally built church buildings),
but they organized churches. It became normative for churches to
have a constitution, by-laws, canons, or governance books (Order

or Discipline). They organized themselves into lay leadership teams, standing committees, and ad-hoc committees. They formed women's groups and men's groups and youth groups. They learned to staff churches with specialists focused on various programs or ministries of this church. They designed and implemented budgets to guide the financial resources of the church. So much that we take for granted now was developed during this era. The gifts of the Builder Generation to the church are numerous and rich.

In addition, how to measure the progress of these churches was clearly identified. Looking around at their world, they recognized that size, property, and attendance were ways other organizations evaluated themselves. These measures naturally fit the ethos of the church movement at that time. Now most churches are very clear about these measures. "Buildings, bodies, and budgets," is short-hand for these measurements. "Church members" became the phrase we Christ-followers used to describe ourselves. This phrase in itself simply describes our relationship to our church. On the other hand, an unintended consequence of this organizational development movement in churches is that we began to use this phrase to describe our primary spiritual identity. "I am a church member." Discipleship, or following Jesus Christ, became secondary.

CHAPTER FOUR
THE DEMISE OF MEMBER IDENTITY

This simple contrast quickly raises the difference between being a church member and a disciple. Being a church member is not wrong; it's just lacking. Let's explore how these titles, or more accurately, identity markers are used in scripture.

Member is a Biblical word; being found 45 times in the New Testament (NRSV). Limiting ourselves to the gospels, we find member eight times. Matthew favors this word more than the others, using it seven times. Twice Matthew's gospel uses member to refer to parts of one's body, twice as a way to describe family relationships (members of one's household), and then member appears three times in the well-known passage about relationships in the church. In Matthew 18 member is used in a way that most closely resembles how we use the word in our world. Both Mark and Luke each use member one time. Their usage is the same, referring to a member of Judaism's Council.

The pastoral epistles is where member is used most often in the New Testament, and likely the greatest influence on the church using this word to describe its participants.

> *"For just as the body is one and has many members, and*
> *all the members of the body, though many, are one*
> *body, so it is with Christ. For in the one Spirit we were*
> *all baptized into one body—Jews or Greeks, slaves or*
> *free—and we were all made to drink of one Spirit.*
> *Indeed, the body does not consist of one member but of*
> *many. Now you are the body of Christ and individually*
> *members of it."*
>
> *I Corinthians 12:12-14, 27, NRSV*

This understanding is useful, faithful, helpful, and healthy. These scriptures seem intent on describing the relationship of one to his/her community of faith, in the context of relationship with Christ. It's interesting that all these descriptions are corporate or community oriented. None of them describe individual disciples. So, the New Testament does not even talk about individual Christ-followers apart from their faith community – the Church. "You are the body of Christ, and individually members of it." Membership, as used in scripture, is a beautiful description of an intertwined community-based relationship, all under the Lordship of Christ.

Yet, over time, something happened to this phrase. Church membership devolved into something different than this organic, Biblical use of the term. During the last half of the twentieth century, when great effort was applied to building many organizations in the United States, the word membership came to mean something across our culture. Membership was admired, encouraged, and desired. For a people who knew deprivation, loss, and war, becoming established as members was comforting. The security of membership was worth pursuing in this context.

American society at large valued membership, in the organizational sense of this word. Organizations like Rotary, Civitan, and Scouting flourished. Professional organizations saw their heyday.

This movement in our society drifted into the church, where the concept of membership devolved to a description of one's relationship to an organization, rather than a referent to living relationships. Perhaps this slow shift to understanding membership as an organizational term seems unimportant. At least three insights highlight the dangers of staying with membership as we know it in describing who we are in Christ.

Membership became an organizational term, meaning "the rights and privileges" of membership.
That phrase – "the rights and privileges thereof" – is familiar from very early in my Christian journey. As a young child I can remember it being used to describe who can vote in church conferences. Usually this discussion included someone referring to the Constitution and By-Laws of the church, and even sometimes included someone actually pulling out a paper copy of that very document from some hidden place for quoting.

Membership describes our relationship to many organizations in our lives.
There is nothing unique, in terms of Christian usage, regarding the word member. At any point in time, I'm a member of several organizations. Each year, I receive an invoice from one professional organization, asking me to renew my membership for another year. Each year I go through my mental checklist. Is it worth it? Does this organization represent where I am in this profession? Can I participate this year in this organization? Does

my participation make a difference in this organization? Am I able to pay the membership fee this year? Who of my friends and colleagues will also participate in this organization this year? These questions are familiar to most of us, knowing what it's like to be a member of multiple organizations.

When membership becomes an organizational term, then membership becomes optional.
Over time, our interests shift, and we move away from membership in some organizations. At one time, we believed we would always be involved in this organization. We would have felt insulted if anyone suggested we would move on at some future point. Then we find ourselves joining new organizations; some we never believed we would join. Membership, when one thinks in organizational terms, is fluid and optional.

"Disciple" is also a Biblical word; being found in the New Testament 263 times (NRSV). The breakdown in the gospels looks like this:

Matthew 72

Mark 47

Luke 39

John 77

Jesus used the word often in parables, stories, teachings, with a few examples following.

"Then Jesus summoned his twelve disciples and gave them authority over unclean spirits, to cast them out, and to cure every disease and every sickness."
Matthew 10:1, NRSV

"At that time Jesus went through the grain fields on the Sabbath; his disciples were hungry, and they began to pluck heads of grain and to eat. When the Pharisees saw it, they said to him, 'Look, your disciples are doing what is not lawful to do on the Sabbath,' He said to them, 'Have you not read what David did when he and his companions were hungry?'"

Matthew 12:1-3, NRSV

"Then Jesus said to the Jews who had believed in him, 'If you continue in my word, you are truly my disciples; and you will know the truth, and the truth will make you free.'"

John 8:31-2, NRSV

In terms of frequency alone, the word "disciple" is far more often used to describe Jesus-followers than the word member. Frequency is a poor way to do theological interpretation in many cases (sin is mentioned quite often, but the frequent use of the word is not encouragement to excel). At the same time, when describing our primary identity, the primary images, words, or metaphors of scripture tell us something about who we are. Though member was used in healthy, encouraging, strengthening ways early on, our culture has co-opted the word for other uses. Besides, the gospels call Christ-followers disciples far more often. Author Brian McLaren describes the Biblical use of disciple this way,

"It's worth noting in this regard that the word 'Christian' occurs in the New Testament exactly three times and the word 'Christianity' exactly zero. The word 'disciple,' however, is found 263 times."[1]

Language Matters, Language Forms Us

Who doesn't appreciate self-deprecating humor? Comedians build careers using the art of putting themselves down. But it's different when in normal conversation we hear another put oneself down. When patterns of derogatory statements about oneself weave through one's conversation, then we hear the lack of self-appreciation. At the same time, the reverse is true. When patterns of self-congratulation permeate one's conversation, we recognize this person is also grasping at ways to feel good about self.

Our language, our talk, our conversation is full of images, metaphors, and descriptions about who we are. These are largely unintentional, yet they are part of how we express ourselves. Language has power to form our very identities.

Contrast the two sets of phrases below

I am a member of this church	I am a disciple of Jesus Christ
I go to church	I am the church
We are the members of this church	We are disciples of Jesus Christ who gather as this church

Over the last five years, I've engaged an experiment. I am trying to eradicate the phrase "church member" from my vocabulary. After being driven back to the scriptures, and considering how membership has morphed over time to mean something different than intended, I became convinced this shift was necessary. Do you know how difficult this has been - and remains? Our church culture in the United States is not designed to accommodate the use of "disciple" to describe Christ-followers.

Given the world wherein we find ourselves now, weak and impoverished descriptions won't suffice. In the Postmodern environment, simply describing my relationship to an organization lacks power. In order to live a robust spiritual journey, I need a robust spiritual identity. Now we need stronger, more invigorated language to help form our identities as Christ-followers. Living as a disciple of Jesus Christ is a powerful calling toward living the ways and teachings of Jesus. Picturing ourselves living as church members, leaves us lacking and slightly bored.

We were discussing this movement, from membership to discipleship, in the seminar portion of a Lead Pastor Cohort. I can still remember the look on his face. One very sharp pastor of a sizeable church looked very disturbed. As I noticed him, I paused the conversation and asked about his thoughts. *"I appreciate what we are talking about and am supportive of this movement. But I'm keenly aware that this language would scare people in our congregation. Our people are used to thinking of themselves as church members, but being disciples of Jesus Christ....that's a whole other way of thinking and relating which our church people aren't used to."* Nods from some around the room, with curious looks from others.

I appreciated this pastor's honest recognition, along with the humility to share it. He reminded me of another conversation with a very "successful" pastor from another Christian denomination. I have great respect for this pastor, observing his ministry in several churches over time. Yet, in a moment of confessional conversation about disciple-making he shared, "I look back over my 35 year ministry and see that myself and the churches I served were really good at making church members. We were not so good at making disciples."

From WWII to 2000, the tail end of the Modern Period, the church in the United States was engaged in exceptional growth and organizational development. For better or worse, we taught people to be fine church members, with discipleship as a secondary endeavor. Now, in this Postmodern Era and Post-Christian culture, discipleship is necessary to sustain one's faith.

The following is a contrast between member identity and disciple identity, when these are lived-out in our faith communities. These are not exact nor exhaustive lists, more like word association, used to help us understand the differences in these words.

Member Based Faith Community	Disciple Based Faith Community
Sacred or secular identity	Sacred identity
Transient	Permanence
Organizational focus	Relational focus
Institutional advancement	Health of the Body
Professionals provide services	Disciples serve each other
Settled	Sent

Just how do we know when we are pursuing disciple identities as a congregation? One way to discern how much your congregation is focused on membership versus discipleship, is to observe the actions of leadership. In our book on Disciple Development

Coaching, Ircel Harrison and I considered the role of pastoral leaders in developing disciples. Consider this description below, extrapolating to to congregational leaders in general, lay and ordained.

"Pastors who buy into the membership perspective relate to church members in that way. Considerations include who is in and who is out, what membership means or doesn't mean, and especially how to get more members. If the pastor is interested in growing the church, then this means recruiting more members. These pastors consider membership numbers a primary indicator the church is spiritually growing and on track. They may or may not be interested in one's continuing growth after signing up for membership.

Disciple-developing pastors don't think this way. They are focused on helping disciples move forward in following Christ. They invest in individuals and groups in the congregation for the purpose of encouraging movement toward Christian maturity. They see the activities of the church as tools for strengthening, initiating, and inspiring disciple development. In some ways church membership becomes a minor factor for these pastors. They are interested in one's development throughout the Christian journey. They see developing disciples as an essential and central focus of their ministries. When disciples are developing, most likely they are far more invested in the church as an organization. Membership can come and go, but discipleship is an expression of who we are."[2]

The Pathway to Faith For Postmodern Pilgrims
When we come to understand how the Modern Era has shaped church-as-we-have-known-it, examples seem to appear before our eyes. As I drove through a suburban town near where I live, I

saw the new campus of a large church which recently moved out of the city to this growing suburb.

Believe – Become – Belong

These three words were prominently displayed on the attractive new sign, just below the church's name. This sign, in front of the new church building, is located on a high volume highway in a busy part of town. When I saw it for the first time recently, I couldn't believe my eyes. There it was, right there on a sign for all to see. Not three weeks before, no fewer than three clergy cohorts discussed this very progression. Our topic was how spiritual seekers enter into faith and church life in this Post-Christian, Postmodern world in which we find ourselves.

We know the typical way people entered faith and church life in the 20th century Christian culture during the Modern Era. For those who came to faith and church involvement beyond their infancy, then the typical progression began with intellectual assent to a body of beliefs (theology and doctrine). Then they "became" Christians through their belief and baptism. Then these pilgrims were welcomed into full membership of this church, "belonging" as church as members. This linear process was more normative than not up until, well, until it was no longer normative.

Now, in this Post-Christian culture with its Postmodern 21st century perspective, this linear progression is not the norm anymore. First of all, people wonder why we would expect them to believe this theology and doctrine we say is true, just because we say it is so. What makes it truer than all the other faith options which claim the same level of truth? There are many competing

worldviews and belief systems available – each including people
we respect and see as admirable.

The cultural norms reinforcing our theology and doctrine in the
20th century are no longer present. Rarely will 21st-century
spiritual seekers begin their entry into the church through
believing first. They have not been prepared by their families, nor
by their culture at large, for belief in the Christian story.

So, how do Postmodern spiritual seekers enter church life? Is
there a typical or normative route? Can we line up the words like
we used to, with any credibility or reliability?

Yes and no. The verdict is still out on what is now normative, since
we are barely into this new century. But a trend seems to be
emerging.

Experience – Belong – Become – Believe

I heard tell of a large church needing a new drummer for its praise
band. They were focused on quality, so they hired a gifted
musician. This young adult was not a Christ-follower, but was
open to playing for worship services after he completed his sets at
clubs on Saturday nights. Predictably, after about a year, he
became really tired, burning the candle on both ends of Saturday
night. In conversation with his wife, he shared his need for a rest,
intending to quit one of these gigs. She quickly said, "Quit the
clubs." He was surprised at her suggestion, since she had no
personal investment in the church job (not a Christ-
follower)."Why?" he asked. "Because I like you so much better
since you started playing in that praise band." After brief
reflection this young man responded, "You know, I think I'm one

of them now. I think I've become one of those Christ-follower people."

First, Postmodern people need to experience Christ through real live people before they can move toward belief. When they experience this genuine integrated faith, observing Christ-followers giving themselves in love for the good of the world, then they think there may be something to the gospel. Then they are interested in participating with this group. After experiencing this group actually loving one another (New Commandment), then they come to identify with the group (belong). This genuine love they experience is convincing, leading to a growing awareness that something real is happening here. Then these Postmodern seekers find they too are growing a bit more loving, authentic and genuine (become).

Thus, the opportunity to believe unfolds. Based on this experience, on belonging with this group (church), and becoming a different person, one grows willing to risk that Jesus Christ is real and trust these beliefs (theology and doctrine). The outcome is the same (faith in Christ), but the predictable pathway we plaster on signs is all a-jumble.

Wow. What are the ramifications of this for church life as we know it? Are we ready for the 21st century as Christ-followers who gather together in groups (churches)? Ready or not, here we go.

CHAPTER FIVE
THE RISE OF DISCIPLE IDENTITY

Remember the three questions? They did not literally save my life, but it sure does seem like they did. I guess I'm not much different than many Christ-followers at the tail-end of the Modern Era. My version of Christianity ran out of energy. When Christendom's demise came along, my interior spiritual life reflected this demise. The experience was like moving into the wilderness with the Hebrews after the Exodus. After a few years, the journey became grueling. Now, I'm so thankful for those three questions which drew me into the pursuit of a new way of being Christian. The first two questions are at the heart of this move from member identity to disciple identity.

What does it mean to be a disciple of Jesus Christ?
What does it mean to live in the Way of Jesus? What does it mean to live as a disciple of Jesus Christ now, in this Postmodern context? This is a captivating question for those of us who follow Jesus. When a person orients his or her life around Jesus Christ, how does this person live? What does this person do? How does a disciple live out discipleship?

To my great surprise and relief, I found there were other Christ-followers fed up with being church members, yet were captivated by Jesus Christ. They too could not walk away from Christ. They too read the gospels and find the Way of Jesus compelling.

Danger Ahead
Before moving on, I have to warn you.
If we really engage this first question (no REALLY), our lives will be rocked. This is so important, with so much potential for changing our lives that I must to warn you in two specific ways.

First, if you think you already know the answers to this question, then you are misunderstanding the significance of this question.

I remembered one of those late night college dorm room conversations with a bunch of guys. I went to Carson-Newman College in East Tennessee, so some were there because it was a good Baptist school. One late night, we were sitting around discussing the meaning of life. Somehow we moved onto a discussion about what it means to really live as a Christ-follower. I remember one guy, from a small town in East Tennessee, describing his understanding…"Many of the people I grew up with were Christians. We had a big youth group and there were lots of Christians at school." Some of us who were not from a setting like this asked, "What was it like? How did being a Christian make people different?" He thought for moment and then said, "Well, I guess I really couldn't tell. Everyone in this small town was pretty nice, and honest, and friendly. You couldn't really see any difference between the Christians and those who weren't." What my friend was describing is cultural Christianity.

I'm so thankful for the impact the Christian movement has made in the United States, influencing values and customs in the larger culture. Simultaneously, many of us are concerned about this tepid version of Christianity perceived to describe faithful Christian experience. Being nice, honest, and friendly are great actions, yet they are mild parts of our faith when we listen to Jesus' teachings.

If you think that's it....then I must warn you to stay away from the Bible. If that's your picture of being a Christ-follower, then do not open the New Testament. For there you will find pages and pages describing how Jesus lived. You will find passages filled with Jesus painting the picture of his way of life. You will read things like the Sermon on the Mount, where Jesus said radical, life-altering statements. Forgive others when they wrong you, and then forgive them some more. Jesus said things like don't be caught up in the pursuit of wealth over more important things in life; they will end up owning you rather than you being a steward of wealth. Jesus encouraged his followers to love their enemies, pray for them, and share with them. Jesus told them not to be overly religious with long prayers, but to concentrate on the simple, more weighty stuff of life. Jesus encouraged his followers to become internally pure rather than trying to look good on the outside. Jesus asked his followers to live from a foundation of compassion, loving others the way we hope to be loved. Wow. Jesus was a far more radical prophet and teacher than his world had ever seen....so much so that they wouldn't tolerate him, executing him instead. There is no way we can follow Jesus without living in direct contrast to the culture around us.

> *"At the same time, the churches have become so*
> *accommodated to the American way of life that they are*
> *now domesticated, and it is no longer obvious what*

justifies their existence in particular communities. The religious loyalties that churches seem to claim and the social functions that they actually perform are at odds with each other. Discipleship has been absorbed into citizenship."[1]

This statement was written by Stanley Hauerwas and William Willimon way back in 1989 when Christendom was still intact, though beginning to crumble. If it was true back then, churches who engage this first question now will find their reality disturbed. When congregations believe they basically have it all together, they are on a slippery slope toward mistaking Jesus for socially sanctioned cultural norms.

Second warning: If you think you will come out on the other side of this question basically the same, then you are underestimating the magnitude of this question.

A few years ago there was a fad that swept across the Christian world – WWJD. Do you remember that? Did you own a yellow wrist-band with WWJD imprinted on it? Charles Sheldon wrote a fictional book from his home in Kansas describing how residents of that small town might live if they asked, "What Would Jesus Do?" before they took action. His book, *In His Steps*, has remained a Christian classic for years.[2] When the WWJD fad really accelerated, I wanted to rush up to Christians who were promoting it and caution them. I wanted to say, "Hey, wait a minute. Do you realize what you are doing by asking people to ask what Jesus would do? Are you actually prepared to live like Jesus?" The vast majority of us underestimate how radical and life-changing following Jesus becomes. When we center our lives in Jesus Christ; when Jesus becomes the organizing principle of our lives, then there is no way life can remain the same.

Robin Meyers describes the risks of discipleship well in his book, *Saving Jesus From The Church.*

> *"His invitation was not to believe, but to follow. Since it was once dangerous to be a follower of The Way, the church can rightly assume that it will never be on the right track again until the risks associated with being a follower of Jesus outnumber the comforts of being a fan of Christ. Until we experience Jesus as a 'radically disturbing presence,' instead of a cosmic comforter, we will not experience him as true disciples. The first question any churchgoer should be asked and expected to answer is: What are you willing to give up to follow Jesus?"[3]*

So if you don't want your world rocked, then don't engage this first question about living as a disciple. None of us can walk away from authentic engagement with Jesus unchanged. If you need things to remain as they are, or have a high need for social conformity, or don't think love has power, or prefer comfort over authentic life, or treasure things over life transformation, then avoid this conversation any way you can. Consider yourself warned.

Appendix 3 – Article: Warning

What does it mean to be a gathered community of Christ followers?

What does it mean to live as a community gathered around Jesus? When several of these Jesus followers get together, collectively deciding to live in the way of Jesus, how do they do it? How do they organize themselves? How do they talk with each other? What do they do? When they put their money together, what do they do with it? How do they help each other live as disciples? What's it look like when Jesus followers form community and sacred partnerships?

Since confession is good for the soul, I want to speak just for me right now. If I risk asking the first question mentioned above with any level of authenticity or depth, I am going to need some help. I have asked this question before. In fact the last 4 or 5 years I've been asking it each year. And you know what I've determined? I can't sustain pursuing an answer by myself. I have to have some partners in on it with me in order to keep going.

And here is why. Allow me to digress with an illustration for a moment. Over the holidays, during that stretch of time between Thanksgiving and New Year, the average American gains 7 pounds. Then comes a new year, along with New Year resolutions. Health clubs relish this time of year, given the reformers who are ready to strap on their new running shoes or exercise gear and hit the gym. But we know what happens in late January and early February. The weather is still cold, it's dark early in the morning when we head to the gym, and the newness of our fitness goals is long gone. Many allow the New Year's resolution to become ancient history at this point.

But there are some who persevere and continue to improve their health. Do you know who these people are? They are the ones who are part of a group focused on the mission of improved health. Those who partner with others around fitness goals are usually those who continue to make progress. The support found through relational connection around the goals provides energy for persevering. They too have a group to celebrate with when progress is achieved.

So, I have to tell you, that if I'm going to live as a Christian disciple, I need some help, and I suspect that you will too. The primary way God answers this need for support is to put us in groups called churches. An age-old question voiced by a Biblical character long ago applies here, "Am I my brother's keeper?" (meaning sister or brother). And the answer when it comes to a Christian community, seeking to authentically follow Jesus, is YES. We need each other to keep up our spiritual vigor, to remain focused on the goal, for courage to ask the hard questions, in order to give up the comforts of this world for the good of this world, we will need each other. We will need support when we fail or are blind to the Way. We will need challenge from each other when we are headed in the wrong direction.

Again, to my delight, I discovered plenty of other Christ-followers who could not tolerate doing church anymore. They were intent on being the church, becoming the church, and contributing to the evolution of the church. I discovered there were movements underway within traditional churches and in new faith communities where this pursuit is primary. How do we love one another (New Commandment) and make disciples of ourselves and others (Great Commission)? This movement, gathered around these two questions, is life giving. That's how these two questions (along with the third previously described) saved my spiritual life.

Christian Formation
As disciples in congregations grow more serious about discipleship, they find themselves questioning their Christian formation practices. Does what we do form disciples of Jesus

65

Christ? Is our Sunday School program designed to support and challenge us sufficiently? Are we engaging in what is needed to follow Jesus Christ in today's world? Are our small groups robust enough to form Christ-followers?

Whether we are aware of it or not, there is always a theory guiding what we do. During two-thirds of the twentieth century, a particular learning theory drove educational efforts in our society. Education systems rested on the belief that accurate and sufficient information is what's needed to live effectively. In other words, knowing information equips a person to do their vocation.

For better or worse, the church adopted this viewpoint, designing its Christian formation activities with this theory as guidance. Traditional Sunday School classes reflected traditional classroom approaches. We believed that when we could gain sufficient information (knowledge), then we would change and live more like Jesus taught and modeled (personal transformation). Correct knowledge leads to life-transformation, was our guiding principle.

In the last third of the twentieth century, multiple intelligences became a popular term. Fortunately, wise educators called us to a wider, fuller view of learning. Yes, knowledge is important. Yet by itself, knowledge is insufficient for compelling change in most of us. We need more. Change and transformation come through accurate knowledge learned through multiple modalities, application, combined with supportive relationships encouraging us to continue the learning or formation process.

CHAPTER SIX
THE DISCIPLE DEVELOPMENT MOVEMENT

Christian Education, Christian Formation....these terms sufficed for a while. Perhaps they were descriptive and helpful during their time. But can we retire them now? Over time words collect meanings, becoming heavy with unforeseen attachments or unintended associations. Now we need new words to describe what we are pursuing when it comes to following Jesus Christ.

What is it we are really trying to do in the church? What is our unique role in the world? Those questions are too large to fully answer here, yet one aspect of the church's commission is clear – to make disciples. Becoming a disciple of Jesus Christ is a life-long endeavor. We start the journey at some point, yet we never complete this journey until the end of all things. So, the Church is tasked with helping people move ahead in this journey. This is the disciple development function of church. I'm trying to change my language again. If we are not church members, but are disciples instead, then we are not doing Christian Education or even Christian Formation, we are trying to develop ourselves and others as disciples. We are cultivating a Disciple Development Movement in our congregations.

No longer christian education or christian Formation, but Disciple Development

Rule of Life

As congregations consider their disciple development efforts, they often find they do not have clear pathways for developing themselves as disciples. Every church does something to develop disciples, yet few are clear and intentional enough; encouraging discipleship movement.

This dilemma is giving rise to the disciple development movement. A fascinating expression of focused development for disciples is the Rule of Life. Those familiar with this phrase recognize it as an ancient practice within the larger Christian movement. Now some faith communities are reaching into Christian history, drawing forward the practice of a Rule of Life. Engagement with this ancient Christian practice is one expression of the move from member identity to disciple identity.

Marjorie Thompson, of The Upper Room, introduces us to Rule Of Life in this description from her book *Soulfeast:*

> *"A rule of life is a pattern of spiritual disciplines that provide structure and direction for growth in holiness. When we speak of patterns in our life, we meant attitudes, behaviors, or elements that are routine, repeated, regular....A rule of life is not mean to be restrictive, although it asks for genuine commitment. ....It fosters gifts of the Spirit in personal life and human community, helping to form us into the persons God intends us to be."[1]*

Long ago, during the medieval period, bands of Christ-followers would gather and form specialized Christian communities. Sometimes they were cloistered, set apart from more typical society. Other times their mission included serving in and among society, meeting particular needs. Some of the great Christian mystics started these specialized communities, while others grew out of the practice of their communal life. As they gathered, the founder would typically articulate a "Rule of Life," a set of guiding principles for this faith community existing within the larger Church. St Francis gave birth to the Franciscans, St Benedict started the Benedictine community, etc. These monastic communities practiced their Rule of Life as a way to become shaped for living in the Way of Jesus Christ.

Monastics....New Monasticism

Now a new monasticism is underway. New faith communities, focused on living in the Way of Jesus, are springing up around this country (and around the world – largely in post-Christian societies). These are bands of (mostly) young adults forming new communities of Christian disciples who are seriously trying to live in the Way of Jesus Christ. Like the ancient monastics, these new faith communities also articulate their guiding principles which function like a Rule of Life for their communal life.

Is this new monasticism a reaction to the state of the church or is it a calling toward a preferred future? Yes. Frustration with the church as we know it partially drives these disciples to start something new. They read the gospels, then examine the church, finding themselves frustrated with the complacency, apathy, and low effort attempts to live in the Way of Jesus Christ. This frustration drives them to seek something new. At the same time, in this process, many of these new faith communities are drawn to the burned-out, blighted, passed over places in major cities. Many of them read about Jesus' great concern for the poor and marginalized, along with Jesus' call to do something about poverty, finding themselves drawn toward action. Based on this, they locate themselves (move to) in sketchy parts of the city, setting up home and hearth among the marginalized and looked-over. Others hearing this same siren song join them, forming new monastic-type communities.

My first exposure to new monasticism came while reading Mark Scandrette's *Soul Grafitti*, published in 2007.[2] He and his family moved from the Midwest to a less-than-desirable part of San Francisco, determined to live in the Way of Jesus in their part of the city. Part of their journey included the formation of a new Christian community (sort of like a church, and sort of not) called Seven. Their faith community gathers around seven themes from how Jesus lived and what he taught:

1. Service
2. Simplicity
3. Creativity
4. Obedience
5. Prayer
6. Community
7. Love

These seven themes functioned in similar ways to the Rule of Life for ancient monastic communities. They are guiding principles around which they build their lives, individually and collectively. Their goal is to help one another live into these themes to the best of their ability, with God's help.

Since that first exposure, I learned there were new monastic-like communities rising up simultaneously in various locales around this country. These were not coordinated efforts, but more like independent mini-movements. With time, they began discovering one another. Through the internet and social media these new faith communities connected, discovering their common mission, language, and ethos.

Eventually there was a gathering of leaders and participants in this "new monasticism," in Durham, North Carolina, resulting in a fascinating description. The participants identified twelve "Marks of a New Monasticism," which they appeared to share. The "marks" themselves include nurturing a common life, sharing resources with one another and the community around them, peacemaking, and living a disciplined contemplative life. Shane Claiborne's *The Irresistible Revolution* lists them in Appendix 2, a book describing the theology and ethos of many of these new monastic communities (See them in this book's Appendix 4)[3]. Claiborne's faith community is The Simple Way in Philadelphia. Jonathan Wilson-Hartgrove, was actually the convener of this group of new monastics who identified their 12 marks. He describes them too, along with the journey of Rutba House in Durham, North Carolina in his book *New Monasticism: What It Has To Say To Today's Church*, published in 2008.[4]

When I first discovered this ancient-new movement around practicing a Rule of Life, I was very encouraged, and very frustrated. Discovering this new monastic movement, especially initiated by the young among us, gives great hope for the Christian Church. There are those who have found the pearl of great price and are willing to leave everything for the sake of the kingdom of God. There are those who are giving careful thought to what it means to be a disciple in our current world, taking action on their insights. This is inspiring and encouraging.

But what about traditional churches or more typical sorts of persons who are Christ followers? Does every disciple need to get up, move somewhere, and start a new life (literally, not only metaphorically)? Are there any traditional type churches engaging the Way of Jesus enough to practice a Rule of Life?

With great joy, I discovered a book the Lutheran pastors in our area were reading and suggesting to each other. Michael Foss, who pastored Prince of Peace Lutheran Church in Minneapolis, wrote up that church's experience with a set of guiding principles. Never did they call this practice a Rule of Life. Instead they described this movement as practicing the Six Marks of Discipleship. In fact that is the name of the ensuing book by Foss, *Six Marks of Discipleship For A Changing Church*, 2000.[5] After much consideration, Prince of Peace Church committed themselves to living out these Six spiritual disciplines.

1. Pray daily
2. Worship weekly
3. Read the Bible
4. Serve at and beyond Prince of Peace
5. Be in relationship to encourage spiritual growth in others
6. Give of my time, talent, and resource

Perhaps these marks of discipleship are not so radical or counter-cultural as those of the new monastics, yet they are movement toward intentional disciple development in a traditional, denominationally based congregation. Their intention was to allow these spiritual disciplines to shape their individual and communal spiritual journeys.

The organization which I lead, Pinnacle Leadership Associates, does congregational consulting around a variety of items – with visioning and discernment processes being a primary focus. Our process includes many activities designed for listening and discernment. In recent years, through many consultations with congregations from various denominations, we are noticing a rising theme. We are hearing and seeing an intense hunger for deep, substantive disciple developing activity. Disciples in these largely traditional kinds of churches, well connected to their denomination, express a yearning for faith-based conversation, for honest spiritually-oriented sharing, and for supportive relationships around their efforts to live in Christ-like ways. I find myself thinking that surely this desire has been present in Christian churches for centuries. But strangely, this desire appears to have gone into hyper-drive, producing great spiritual hunger for living in the Way of Jesus. It seems that the spiritual hunger driving younger people to new monastic communities in the inner cities is the same spiritual hunger permeating traditional churches. Christ-followers are not content with church-as-we-have-known-it. They yearn for deeper, significant, faith-laced spiritual interaction and engagement.

Now we are finding that some of these churches are lighting up when they learn about a Rule of Life. Yes, traditional type churches can and are identifying their Rule of Life, endeavoring to shape their Christian experience around it. The following are examples of churches with whom we have worked who are engaged with a Rule of Life as a guiding force in their disciple development movement.

Church 1 – United Methodist – Rule of Life

- Worshipping God weekly
- Praying and reading scripture daily

- Engaging in a Christian formation-focused small group
- Giving generously of my time, talent, and treasure
- Sharing my faith story with those ready to hear
- Serving vigorously, making a difference in the world

The following is a description of how this church planned to implement their Rule of Life into their culture and practice of the Faith.

- We will adopt this Rule of Life as the beginning place for Christian discipleship for its members
- We will intentionally and consistently practice this Rule of Life until it becomes part of the our culture
- We will use this Rule of Life as a way to communicate the practice of discipleship in our community to new and prospective disciples
- We will develop a church-wide Christian formation experience which integrates worship, Sunday School, other Small Groups around this Rule of Life for a specific period of time (Six – Eight Weeks) to help us launch our Rule of Life

Church 2 – Episcopal – Rule of Life

The priest and lay leaders in this church shared that some in their congregation know what Rule of Life means, being familiar with the monastic tradition. Simultaneously, this church includes many who are newer to the Christian faith, with little familiarity with a ROL. They feared disciples in their context would mistake a ROL to mean Rules For Life. To clarify the meaning, to make clear this is a way of living or practices designed to form us, they added this introductory phrase:

"Our pathway to a deeper relationship with Christ"

- Pray daily
- Worship weekly
- Read the Bible
- Serve others
- Share your story
- Give freely

Implementation method: Forming new small groups who use a curriculum written by the Rector. Publicizing everywhere (repeatedly) and printing small cards for disciples to carry, use, and give away.

Church 3 – Baptist – Living the Disciple Life 2012

This is a church wherein I served as an Interim Pastor for one year, followed by three years as their Renewal Pastor. The desire to go deeper, living more fully as disciples, grew strong in this church. This played out as an invitation to pledge to living the Disciple Life for one year. During the Fall, each of the six activities was explored in a worship service, culminating in pledge Sunday, using the following disciple activities. Disciples were encouraged to commit to all six, yet it was up to each person which activities to pledge toward. This church did not use the terminology "Rule Of Life," yet they were practicing their ROL during this one particular year. You will notice more specificity in this list, given their one-year time frame.

1. Worshipping with other disciples weekly
2. Engaging in an additional Small Group experience
3. Helping others connect to God and God's Church
4. Praying daily for my spiritual journey and for the spiritual journey of this church

5. Serving in at least three missional projects or ministries through this church
6. Growing in my financial giving to God through God's church

I was talking with a pastor of a church which has made significant progress toward becoming a disciple developing congregation. They are focusing on the fruits of the Spirit, noted in Galatians 5:22-23. Here is how they evaluate their disciple development movement. "We ask the disciples who are part of this church, after they've been here for a while, how much they are now disciples of Jesus Christ? More specifically, we ask how much these fruits of the Spirit have increased in their way of living. Our goal is to shift everything in our church experience to support the growth of these fruits in our lives."

Here is how the pastor describes their viewpoint in another church wherein a disciple development movement is underway, "If the disciples in our church are not more Christ-like this year than they were at this time last year, then we are failing each other. Our calling is to encourage, support, and challenge each other in our growth as disciples of Jesus Christ. If we are not seeing the evidence of this growth in our lives, then we are off-track as a church."

As expected when doing something new, there is pushback. It's not been significant, but as we share the Rule of Life concept, some clergy, church staff, and laity react in fearful ways. Three fears in particular are usually expressed in some form among a group being exposed to the Rule of Life.

"We are making following Jesus too hard."
Honestly, I don't know how to raise the bar when it comes to

following Jesus. Statements in the gospels are far more radical than most anything I can imagine. Practicing a Rule of Life is tame compared to the demands of the gospel. If one believes the Rule of Life is too challenging, I would advise avoiding the teachings of Jesus.] *But isn't this what many are choosing?*

"We will scare away potential newcomers to our church if we [Connected more to the ways of the world.] *adopt a Rule of Life."*

How did we ever get to the place where we see practicing our faith as onerous and burdensome? Didn't Jesus say, "Come to me all who are weary and I will give you rest. My yoke is easy and my burden is light." When we orient our lives around Jesus Christ, supported by sacred partnerships, we discover a depth of meaning and significance dripping with life. What is the image those who fear practicing the Rule of Life are seeing?

Contrary to a negative, burdensome experience, those who actually practice spiritual disciplines typically find life therein. The effect is spiritual invigoration, marked by joy. When these disciples practice a Rule of Life corporately, as a congregation, then their sense of community runs deep. They find themselves energized about life in Christ. This is far more attractive to newcomers than what newcomers typically experience among tepid and timid congregations.

"We are not a rules oriented church. We practice grace."
When church leaders express this fear, we know they are misunderstanding the nature of a Rule of Life. They are interpreting "Rule" to mean "rules." The Rule of Life, as used originally in monastic communities and in Postmodern new monasticism, is a way of life. Rule of Life describes practices or principles which we use to craft a life of faith. Rule of Life

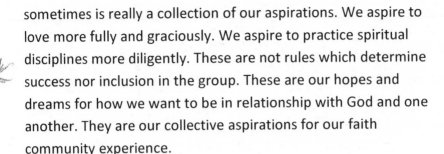

sometimes is really a collection of our aspirations. We aspire to love more fully and graciously. We aspire to practice spiritual disciplines more diligently. These are not rules which determine success nor inclusion in the group. These are our hopes and dreams for how we want to be in relationship with God and one another. They are our collective aspirations for our faith community experience.

At the same time, I appreciate it when I hear people asking these questions. This means they are beginning to recognize we are describing seismic shifts in how we are church. Church-as-we-have-known-it is passing way, while God is making all things new. We are letting go of former paradigms, mental models, and nostalgic memories. Now we are pushing ourselves to embrace a new reality. Sure, we are building the airplane while flying it, yet this is what the Church has always done. We are making the road by walking, to borrow an image. Embracing a Rule of Life as a congregation gives us a way to gain traction for moving ahead into God's future. Identifying and then practicing our Rule of Life is part of making the shift toward becoming a 21st century church. Can we wait any longer? The world needs the Christian gospel as much, or far more than ever. Ourselves and our world cannot wait any longer. The time for making the shift from member identity to disciple identity is now.

CHAPTER SEVEN
MAKING THE SHIFT TOWARD DISCIPLE IDENTITY

Churches can gain great self-awareness when they slow down and listen to themselves. One congregation and its leadership wanted to strengthen its staff through identifying healthy and productive practices for effective staff ministry. During our conversations, the following insights relevant to this church's overall ministry rose to the surface.

1. People in our culture sleep less and work more than previous generations.
2. People in our culture are involved in more recreational activities than ever before, including their children and teens.
3. Both parents work outside the home in most of the two-parent families in our church.
4. Our church is designed for a previous culture, wherein people enjoyed more "discretionary" time.
5. Staff members are feeling pressure to provide more coordination, management of ministries, and program development than ever before (as a result of the above dynamics).

6. Recruiting volunteers to serve in and through the church is increasingly difficult.

This church staff and lay leaders engaging this discussion are not alone. These trends are the waters in which most of us swim.

So how do we respond? If we are institutions which were designed with relevance for previous cultural trends but not for current trends, then what do we do? The bottom line is...we adapt and adjust. We shift how we do what we do so that we can engage people in our culture now, in culturally relevant ways.

There are two healthy ways which churches are adjusting that we recommend for your consideration. First, churches are considering what is essential to being church (Purpose Seeking.) What is it we are really about, and then how do we organize ourselves for that mission? Developing Disciples is typically one of the primary activities churches identify when they do this kind of self-examination. The Church is uniquely tasked with cultivating Christ-followers. God's Church develops disciples.

As disciples are developed churches experience an energy and morale boost. As these rise, then the second healthy adjustment is far easier – letting dying or peripheral programs, ministries, and traditions die. Those in the Baptist tradition, may remember Sunday evening worship services. As Sunday evening services were passing away, many people vehemently argued for continuing them (though they themselves did not attend). What about women and men's programs based on outdated models? We have always (at least in our memories) done it this way. Churches are freeing their energy for doing what's essential, developing Christ-followers.

A nice side-effect of engaging in what is real, meaningful, and mission congruent is the courage to discontinue that which is no longer relevant or substantive. It takes energy to deal with the aftermath (if there is one) of letting go. When churches grow more invigorated, then these changes shrink and become less problematic.

Now let's turn to the disciple development movement in your congregation. We intentionally use the word "movement" to avoid less helpful words, like program or class. We are looking at disciple development as one of the three major streams flowing through a congregation (Big Three Moves). When we grow focused on the purpose of the Church, then developing disciples quickly rises to the top of our list. The following are initiatives which can further the disciple development movement in your congregation.

Cultivating an appetite for Christ-Centered Faith Practices
One of quickest ways for people to move from seeing themselves as church members to this new identity of disciples is to engage Christ-centered faith practices. In fact, engaging Christ-centered faith practices is simply part of what disciples do. They want to engage in activities and actions which will cultivate their identity as disciples.

Classic spiritual disciplines are pathways to disciple development. Some people will gain traction through individually pursuing spiritual disciplines. Perhaps they read Richard Foster, Richard Rohr, or Henri Nowen and decide to practice a form of prayer for a period of time. More often, disciples in this exposure and learning stage will find more success by joining a group focused on the spiritual disciplines. There are many good studies or programs to guide small groups. The obvious advantages of this group approach tend to further the movement; support, encouragement, and accountability.

Another part of engaging spiritual disciplines is to subtly (or overtly) guide disciples away from organizationally oriented activities. Often disciples define their spiritual progress through administrative functions; like serving on a committee or lay leadership teams. Though these may be good and even needed activities, they usually are not foundational activities for strengthening one as a disciple. They may be the result of one's spiritual formation (service), rather than the sum total of one's discipleship. First, engage disciples in spiritual disciplines, then they will serve in ways more congruent with their gift set.

When churches begin intentionally engaging Christ-centered faith practices, it's almost humorous how often these turn out easier than they expected. We human beings carry an innate sense of the spiritual, knowing there is something (and someone) beyond what we see, hear, taste, and smell. With the swift growth of the "Nones" in our society (spiritual but not religious), we are reminded that people want to continue their spiritual quest whether they are religious about it or not. When churches encourage Christ-centered faith practices, they serve up an opportunity for this faith-based spiritual hunger to be satisfied. This is part of our journey as Christ-followers.

Identifying and Implementing Your Rule of Life (ROL)
Who is an expert in God? Who in the Christian movement has captured all there is to know and experience about being a disciple? Perhaps those among us who perceive themselves to be experts are the least expert in following Christ. Regardless, there is great breadth and tremendous variety when it comes to the

Christian experience. Given this, the complexity of our faith can be overwhelming. Sometimes recognizing the nuances of our faith can lead to paralysis when it comes to practicing our faith. Our goal in church is not to confuse or overwhelm sincere seekers. Our goal is to help one another gain traction in following Christ. This is the beauty of the ROL, giving disciples focus, clarity, and direction.

Your process for identifying your congregation's ROL will involve much exploration, conversation, and discernment. This is not a simple process, and the importance is significant. Give yourselves time, sprinkled with patience, allowing the ROL to rise up as its ready. Imagine the effect when disciples in your congregation begin this quest to answer the two discipleship questions. What does it mean to be a disciple of Jesus Christ? What does it mean to be a gathered community of disciples? The classic ROL question is, What practices might we engage which will give us the best opportunity to become more mature disciples of Jesus Christ? The exploration and conversation resulting from the pursuit of answers will be invigorating for your congregation.

One decision you will make in the process is how specific to become in your ROL. Some faith communities hold very broad disciplines. "Simplicity," is in the ROL of the Seven Community in San Francisco. Practicing simplicity...there is plenty of room for interpretation in this, yet it gives direction for spiritual engagement. Other faith communities choose far more specific disciplines, like "worshipping God weekly." Little interpretation is needed to take action, implementing this ROL.

This ROL exploration, identification, and then pursuit is a game changer for congregations. The previous approach to welcoming

new disciples into the congregation was primarily propositional.
This was the basic congregational entry conversation:
"Do you believe what we believe?"
"Yes"
"Have you been baptized as a Christ follower?
"Yes"
"Then come on in and join us."
"OK. What now?"

The ROL gives you a very specific answer to the "what now?"
question.
"We aspire to live as disciples of Jesus Christ in this way….ROL."
Newer disciples are invited to practice this ROL with you, being
formed as disciples in these ways.

So, the process for identifying and implementing your ROL is
simple. Invite the congregation to set aside a season of time to
explore the two basic discipleship questions. Then introduce ROL
examples from Shift and other resources. This leads to dialogue,
prayer, and discernment about what may be your ROL – your
collective aspirations for living the disciple life. Usually,
congregations need examples with which to begin. As you
explore, at some point, someone(s) will actually put fingers to
keyboard or pen to paper to create a draft. Stay with the process
until you gain consensus for your ROL. As you practice the ROL,
refinement may happen. Get started, go forward, and trust God
to be active in the process.

Initiate, Invigorate, and Engage Disciple Developing Small Groups
Looking back, archeologists tell us that human beings have always
demonstrated a propensity to gather themselves in groups. Our
ancient ancestors were tribal people, gathering in groups, clans,

and communities – like we do to this day.

If you don't believe it, just go with my freshman-in-high-school daughter for a day. You would walk down the hallway and see preppies, jocks, and nerds. You could see students who are part of the Goth group, or the drama club, or musicians, or technical geeks. You will see t-shirts with college and professional team logos for many sports. Everyone is clearly identifying themselves with some group, or in opposition to some group, displaying their identity markers.

We adults are just the same. The next time you drive through town, pay attention to the bumper stickers and magnets on the back and side of peoples' cars, mini-vans, and SUVs. They proclaim our connection to the Dance Department, to our children's school, political parties, or our college Booster Club.

There is something deep within us as human beings which drives us to connect with others in community. When it comes to developing disciples, our DNA driven impulse toward community gives us clues on how to move ahead. Gathering disciples in small groups, focusing on disciple development, provides a powerful context for cultivating disciple identity.

Most churches have observed by now that those newcomers who become part of a small group within the larger church are the ones who stick. Those who only engage in worship, as important as this is, rarely become involved with the faith community in deeper ways and often don't stay with the church.

Launching, or renewing your small group ministry involves two actions. These can be done simultaneously, the first giving good cause for engaging the more difficult second. First, churches can launch new disciple developing small groups for the purpose of engaging their Rule of Life. One church with whom we worked launched their Rule of Life and disciple developing small group ministry simultaneously. For eight weeks, worship focused on one of their ROL practices. During those same eight weeks disciples were encouraged to join a new small group wherein participants would learn and practice the ROL. As the eight weeks were completed, each small group was encouraged to continue gathering, practicing disciple development. It's very likely that your congregation will need plenty of new small groups which are focused on developing disciples.

The second action is a review or assessment of your current small groups. We are suggesting *disciple developing small groups.* This means they are more than social, service, or any other kind of group. These are groups specifically focused on engaging spiritual disciplines (Bible Study, prayer, ROL) with each other. These are groups which provide support, encouragement, and accountability for living out one's calling as a disciple. The curriculum and content can vary, yet the focus remains disciple development. Your congregation likely has many small groups. Some of them are not really disciple developing. Of these, engaging a review with an eye toward disciple development, will give the opportunity to decide whether they are helpful to your congregation's mission.

Engaging Disciple Development Coaching© and Spiritual Direction
How is the disciple care ministry in your church organized? Some churches still use the exclusive phrase "pastoral care." Many others broaden their terminology to member care, or now, disciple care. This is another way I'm working to change my

vocabulary. Since we are disciples, and since more people than only pastors can serve in caring ministries, I'm calling this area of church life "disciple care." Whatever your congregation currently calls this, how are the care needs met in your congregation? Who, in addition to your clergy, are engaged in this ministry? Most congregations have a formal or informal way of addressing the care needs of disciples when they arise.

As sophisticated and proactive as we are regarding disciple care, we are rarely so intentional about developing disciples (one of the primary mandates of the church). We are suggesting that even with a robust small group disciple developing ministry, there is another disciple developing need to be addressed. There are individuals in every congregation, who with some encouragement, are ready to grow and develop as disciples. If someone would simply reach out to them and invite them into relationship around their spiritual growth, they would be thrilled.

This is the purpose of two forms of ministry. First, Disciple Development Coaching© is a process for pairing two individuals together for disciple growth. Our book *Disciple Development Coaching: Christian Formation For the 21st Century,* co-authored with Ircel Harrison, covers this ground quite well. DDC trains a cadre of people in a congregation to do Disciple Development Coaching. Then they are paired with those who are ready to move ahead in their discipleship, discovering and living out their callings at a much higher level. This Disciple Development Coaching book lays out how to initiate and develop a movement in your congregation. The second ministry to consider is spiritual direction. There are many fine training programs around the country which can equip spiritual directors to serve effectively. These one-on-one relationships provide great opportunity for disciples to accelerate their growth for a season.

Integrating Your Clear Ongoing Disciple Development Process
When are we finished being formed as disciples of Jesus Christ?
It's not over until it's over (in the ultimate sense). We are always a
work in progress, with more room to grow. So every congregation
needs ways to continue the journey.

What's next? When disciples in our faith community ask this
question, we need a way to discover the answer. When a disciple
completes a time-limited small group, finishes a series of spiritual
direction conversations, or is simply ready to intentionally move
ahead in spiritual growth, then we need ways to discern the next
steps. This part of shifting toward the disciple identity can't be
programmed. Instead this is the organic part of Christian
formation. The faith community provides structure and ministries
which help us move toward discipleship. At some point though
the next step becomes very individualized. This is when disciples,
in conversation with spiritual guides or disciple developers, may
discover avenues of disciple development yet to be dreamed.

PART THREE
ATTRACTIONAL CHURCH TO
MISSIONAL CHURCH

The Church Growth Movement was running full speed in the 1980s, with great traction among clergy, seminaries, and denominations. One outcome from this movement was the seeker-oriented church. These churches organized themselves around their understanding of spiritual seekers, not-yet-Christians, and their spiritual quest. This resulted in welcoming buildings with little spiritual imagery or religious artwork, fearing too much Christian imagery may scare seekers away. Typically, worship in these seeker-oriented settings included contemporary music, with a lengthy sermon on how to live a better life, based on one's faith in Jesus Christ.

During this time, my father was coaching many church planters or new church developers. I remember hearing him quote one church planter who was several years into a successful new church launch, designed with seekers in mind. "We are always one week away from failure." This church planter made this remark with great fatigue in his demeanor and expression, in addition to a fair amount of anxiety.

The candor and honesty from this successful new church developer was striking and insightful. When a church's goal is to attract people to what it is doing, market research, marketing techniques, and even worship can become driven by what will attract greater numbers. Keeping them after they come is an ongoing challenge, accompanied by the weekly pressure of having to produce an even better show come Sunday. Though this example is extreme compared to most traditional churches, it does illustrate some dilemmas inherent in the attractional church model.

CHAPTER EIGHT
THE DEMISE OF THE
ATTRACTIONAL CHURCH

Alan Roxburgh and Scott Boren, missional church experts, say that 90% of the churches in North America are attractional churches. The vast majority of our churches are designed to get people to their campus so that these spiritual seekers can find what they are looking for, even when they don't know they are looking for it.

Earlier (Contexting) we described some of the sociological factors which supported the Age of Christendom. Toward the end of the twentieth century was the last extension of Christendom's reach. The best description I've found of this attractional church paradigm is given by Roxburgh and Boren. They remind us of "The Field of Dreams" movie released in 1989 starring Kevin Costner. One of the lines often quoted after this popular movie's debut is "If you build it, they will come." Attractional churches are driven by this belief. When we build attractive buildings, with great programming, engaging worship, and excellent welcome teams….then many people will come to our church campus for events. In other words, if we can get them here, then perhaps we can keep them here, and then we are a successful or effective church. The driving force behind the attractional church is a belief that greater numbers in worship and our programs is the indicator that God is blessing us. The energy in attractional churches is consciously and unconsciously tied up in this drive – to increase numbers in everything we are doing. Remember, Roxburgh and Boren say that 90% of churches in North America are attractional churches.[1]

For many of us, describing church in this way is unsettling. We are bothered by the assumption that numbers drive our church experience. On the other hand, are we saying that being an attractional church is spiritually bankrupt or terribly wrong? Are we discounting what the church has done for years? Roxburgh and Boren say it well,

> *"Let us be clear: we do not intend to attack or to denigrate being attractive in what a church does. No one should plan a worship event or program unless it's attractive. ..Neither of us would be content to lead a church that intentionally repels people because we have some ideal vision of being missional. We are not advocating an either/or imagination that demands that we move from attractional to missional. That would be a sign of poor leadership. We are simply saying that the attractional pattern is not the goal or the primary call of the church."[2]*

So being an attractional church is not wrong or bad, it simply is not the primary focus of the gospel (we will return to this thought soon). Of course we don't believe that the Christian movement's goal is to get big numbers to events. Is this what the incarnation of Jesus Christ was about – to get people to our churches? No, the incarnation of Jesus Christ was about bringing the kingdom of God to earth, establishing it, and helping it to flourish. We are about God's kingdom coming on earth, as it is in heaven.

Laying aside theology for a moment, there is a basic assumption underlying the attractional church model, followed by significant corollary assumptions.

Attractional Church's Primary Assumption – People are looking for a church, either consciously or unconsciously. Therefore, our goal is to become as attractive as possible (Thanks again to Roxburgh and Boren).[3]

Perhaps there was some validity to this assumption between 1940 and 1980. After WWII, the North American expression of the church experienced unprecedented growth. The Builder generation added its savvy and determination to the mix, leading to well organized and numerically growing churches. This was the age of Christendom continuing its cultural movement.

During this time, being part of a church was socially acceptable, or even desirable. Many encouraging motivations led people to join churches. I was consulting with one very established church in a relatively small Southern U.S. community, when I heard one person on a team with whom I was working make the statement, "I'm so tired of local and state politicians who live in this area joining our church and then never showing up again." She recognized what used to be the case in much of America; one needed to be a church member to get elected to public office. During the Age of Christendom, this was the cultural standard.

Given this, the church as a whole developed an organizational self-perception. Constitutions and by-laws were required by governments to establish a church as a non-profit organization. This also requires that a leadership group, or board, with trustees be established. Satisfying the legal requirements was one factor contributing to our self-perception as organization (rather than organism). Many additional factors contributed to this self-focus. Suffice it to say that the church's goal became to attract persons to the church campus and membership.

Along with this primary assumption (the general public is looking for a good church home) are corollary assumptions driving activity in attractional churches.

When we do church with quality and excellence, then people will come to our church.
"If we can just call a young pastor, who is married and has three children of various ages, then we will draw more young people to our church." I wouldn't discourage a church from doing so, yet I've coached many pastors and churches who find themselves discouraged, or even in conflict, when the expected outcome doesn't happen. So they tinker with the system, making improvements here and there, raising the quality of what they do. When the underlying assumption is the problem (believing people are looking for a church), then working the corollaries leads to frustration.

Attractive buildings open the door for those looking for a church like ours.
There is enough truth here to be seductive. I read a research study some years ago describing the top reasons why people worship at a particular church the first time. The top two reasons were an invitation from someone they know or the location of the

church building. Making our buildings attractive is always good. Simultaneously, it is unlikely to return the results we are hoping for, since it too is built on the faulty assumption that many people are looking for a church.

When we get the right programs in place, then people will come to our church.

While consulting at a church recently, an older gentleman pulled me aside after the meeting. He delivered to me his best advice, with great sincerity and conviction, about what will help this church. "If we just get good children and youth programs in place, then we will make it." From his perspective, there is great truth in this statement. In the 1960s and 1970s when his children were young and he and his family joined this church, solid programs were major driving forces in their decision. If there were many people who were now looking for solid children and youth programs in churches for their children, then this would still be so. It's simply not so anymore.

Making progress with buildings, bodies, and budgets is how we know we are doing well.

During the age of Christendom, this is how many measured church effectiveness. When we were building or at least maintaining our campus, when we were increasing the membership roll, and when we were increasing or at least maintaining our budget, then we assumed we were being effective as a church. This belief is centered directly on the sociology underneath the Age of Christendom. When a church is located in a very Christian culture, there are enough Christian-leaning people looking for churches to keep this understanding of church alive.

But what about now, post-2000? Certainly our sociological and cultural context in North America is changed (we will discuss theology soon). We are looking more like Europe in its religious experience every day. The decline of participation in organized religion of any kind is swift and ongoing. This new cultural reality is crisis-creating for established churches and Christian disciples of good faith all across North America. We hear it in churches regularly. Most of the time concern about what's happening is expressed in the form of questions.

"Does God not care about the church anymore?"
"Are our buildings going to become museums, like what happened in Europe?"
"Why isn't God blessing our efforts anymore?"
"This used to work (events, program, quality services). Why isn't it working now (drawing crowds)?"
"Wouldn't we reach more people if we just _____ (fill in the blank with myriads of ideas)?"

So now we are in a state of crisis due to what we see happening around us. This crisis is theological, with people questioning their faith and belief systems. This crisis is methodological, as churches are realizing their paradigm no longer resonates to its former degree with their ministry context. I'm sure there are additional crisis beyond these very obvious ones we have named. Where does this leave God's people and God's church?

What an ideal time to be the church! What an exciting time to be a disciple of Jesus Christ who gathers with others to form a church who is open to the Holy Spirit's wind.

I received an email from an administrator at the seminary,

inquiring if the coming class would be a fitting one for a visiting pastor to take in. This pastor was on campus for a couple weeks, studying and resting, before returning to his congregation in the Washington, DC area. I was teaching a class on Adaptive Leadership, working to prepare seniors at the seminary to lead congregations toward healthy adaptation in their contexts. Certainly we would welcome a pastor from the front lines of ministry into this seminar style class.

At one point during this class, we came to a discussion about Postmodern dynamics and how they are influencing the way we do ministry. That's when this experienced pastor, ministering in an urban and diverse context, spoke up. "I can only speak from my context. But from that perspective, our church finds itself in a situation very similar to the culture and context of the early church. Perhaps more than any other time in the history of the North American church, we are in a setting like our spiritual kin from the first century." The class let this soak in for a moment.... then peppered this pastor with questions about how his church is responding. With candor and grace, he continued to share his experience. As he talked, we could see the great excitement on his face, along with the weariness that comes from significant change efforts.

Yes, that's the story we find ourselves in (thanks Brian McLaren for this useful and fitting phrase). This is a great transition time for us. We are letting go of the former way of being church, following the Holy Spirit into new territory. When we can move with this kind of mindset, with an accurate understanding of what's happening, then we can let go and follow God's lead. What a great time to be the Church.

CHAPTER NINE
THE RISE OF THE MISSIONAL CHURCH

"Necessity is the mother of invention," so they say. It's no accident that the missional church movement is emerging from these crises. When we face challenges, courageously engaging reality as we find it, then we discover new pathways for being church. This is the milieu from which the missional church movement is rising.

One phrase is at the heart of this missional church movement, "Missio Dei," meaning, Mission of God. Yes, God commissioned the church to be and to do. Yet, God was on mission long before the Church began. God continues to be on mission in this world, inviting the Church to join God in this mission. In this way of thinking, the Church is not the primary focus. The mission of God is priority. The Church is a missional partner with God toward transforming the world, partnering to continue the kingdom of God. God's mission is to unveil the kingdom of God, here on earth as it is in heaven. God is working for the healing and reconciliation of this world.

God takes initiative. As far back as the beginnings book (Genesis), we see this poetic description of God hovering over the deep and shaping the very substance of the earth. God takes initiative to create the world, followed by breathing life into humankind. Then throughout salvation history (see Holy Bible), God continues taking initiative; continues reaching out to the world and its human inhabitants. A few examples of God's initiative include:

- Abraham and Sarai being called to leave home and hearth for a "land thy knew not of"
- The entire Exodus story
- The message of the OT prophets – to step out of the comfort zone to join God in bringing justice
- The incarnation of Jesus Christ (The BIG example)
- The sending of the church into the world
- The Diaspora of the early church

These are Biblical examples which illustrate a basic understanding of God for those involved in the missional church movement. These kinds of examples help form the lens through which missional theologians look. Many theologians and practitioners are contributing to the missional church movement. One person (already referenced extensively) who has contributed greatly to this movement is Alan Roxburgh. Nearly any of his books (*Introducing The Missional Church* with Scott Boren and *The Missional Leader* with Fred Romanuk) draw the reader into the Missional Church conversation. Other writers and presenters who have influenced my thinking on the Missional Church are Craig Van Gelder, Alan Hirsch, Darrell Guder, Jonathan S. Campbell, Michael Frost, David Bosch, and Rick Rouse.

"Missional" then, is a way of seeing God, God's movement, and God's kingdom. Missional does not mean a church with a missions committee. Missional is a descriptor of God as described in Scripture. Let's consider this picture of God from Scripture as a missionary, sent God with a church who partners in this mission.

Seeing God as a missionary God
> *"We have learned to speak of God as a 'missionary God.' Thus we have learned to understand the church as a 'sent people.' As the Father has sent me, so I send you (John 20:21)."[1]*
>
> *Darrell Guder*

The examples from Hebrew and Christian history noted above indicate that God takes the initiative. God's biggest move was in the incarnation of Jesus Christ. The life, words, and ways of Jesus gave the world the fullest, most detailed description of God and God's ways. Still, God is on the move through the Holy Spirit. God's mission is not complete until the kingdom comes on earth, as it is in heaven. The missional church recognizes the very character of God includes this great initiative toward the world and its inhabitants. God is a missionary, moving from there to here.

Seeing God as a sending God
Not only does God take great initiative, but God forms others to imitate this initiative.
> *"Mission (is) understood as being derived from the very nature of God. It (is) thus put in the context of the doctrine of the Trinity, not of ecclesiology or soteriology. The classical doctrine of the mission Dei as God the Father sending the Son, and God the Father and the Son sending the Spirit (is) expanded to include yet another "movement": Father, Son, and Holy Spirit sending the*

church into the world."²

David Bosch

Missional theologian David Bosch makes a bold move here. Of course mission work has always been a part of church life, with systematic theologians discussing the missionary impulse in ecclesiology (what the church is and does) and soteriology (how salvation comes to humankind). But Bosch restores the place of mission to none other than the Trinity. Mission first comes from the very nature and character of God, seen through the interaction of the Trinity. This means God is on mission, rather than giving the church primary ownership of the mission. God is on mission, sending Jesus as God's incarnation, followed by the Holy Spirit to carry the mission forward.

Seeing the Church as an instrument of God's mission
Darrell Guder teaches that the church is the instrument of God's mission.

> *"..we have begun to learn that the Biblical message is more radical, more inclusive, and more transforming than we allowed it to be. In particular, we have begun to see that the church of Jesus Christ is not the purpose or the goal of the gospel, but rather its instrument or witness."³*

So God is on mission in the world, inviting the Church to join this mission. This is different than seeing our commission as establishing the Church in the world. No, the mission of God, unleashing God's kingdom...that is the goal. The Church is an instrument for God's work. The Church joins God in the world, uncovering the kingdom.

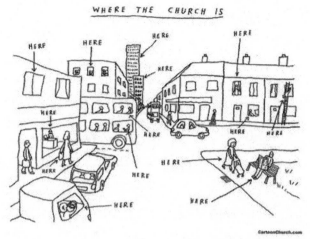

WHERE THE CHURCH IS

Karl Barth For Dummies, Facebook

Without much reflection, we easily see that missional theology shifts the role of the Church from being the goal to being a participant in reaching the objective. The Church's role becomes active partner with God, working to unveil God's kingdom.

When we bring this theology down to where we live, it shifts our great concern about institutional advancement and survival. God is there, and over there, and right here in the world. God calls us there too. The institution of the Church is valuable only as much as it helps move us out the door and into the world. Guder summarizes this perspective well, *"...yet this helpfully highlights the need for and providential appearance of a theological revolution in missional thinking that centers the body of Christ on God's mission rather than post-Christendom's concern for the church's institutional maintenance."*[4]

Seeing the Church as on mission with God in the world, rather than doing missions projects and programs
"In the ecclesiocentric approach of Christendom, mission

became only one of many programs of the church...But it has taken us decades to realize mission is not just a program of the church. It defines the church as God's sent people. Either we are defined by mission, or we reduce the scope of the gospel and the mandate of the church. Thus our challenge today is to move from church with mission to missional church."[5]

So God is on mission in this world. This is the theology permeating the missional church movement. God is not still, or resting, or passive. God is actively engaging the world, pursuing God's mission. Given this, God invites the Church to be on mission with God. The entire Church endeavor is about God's kingdom coming to earth as it is in heaven.

Sometimes a picture is worth a thousand words.

Surely David Hayward at nakedpastor.com was not trying to introduce a graphic to become the official graphic of the missional church movement. But were he, or anyone else to try producing one...

What do we see in this graphic?

From the vantage point of most of us North American Christ-followers, we are used to viewing the world from the first block, an attractional church understanding of God's ways. God is found at church. Then the church does missions. Therefore the church has a mission to accomplish. The second block gives us a visual of the missional church perspective. God is expansive. God preceded the church. God continues the mission God began long before the church was born. The church is an instrument of God's activity for bringing God's reign on earth. The kingdom of God is here and is also coming. The church is one example of the kingdom. Therefore God has a mission to accomplish, and the church is called to join God in that mission.

The following statement would make a great caption for David Hayward's illustration above.

"It is not the church of God that has a mission, it is the God of mission that has a church."

Rowan Williams, Archbishop of Canterbury[7]

Most churches have a mission statement; one which basically reveals a theology based on the first half of William's statement. "Our churches mission is ...." Many good activities or directions are then identified. The missional church movement would suggest a mission statement for churches as something like: "Our mission is to join God on mission in the world," or "Our mission is to join God's movement of restoration and reconciliation in the world." Mission belongs to God. Mission is part of God's nature and character. God invites us (Church) to join God's mission.

The Missional Church movement is off and running. In some ways everything which comes along is a corrective to, or builds upon, what has gone before. The Missional Church movement is no exception. What has preceded this movement (the attractional church model) is a major factor driving this course correction toward God's mission. We can see how our theology can drift toward self-centeredness when Christendom is in vogue.

Now, more of us are recognizing and accepting the fact that our previous sociological assumption(s) no longer apply. The general public in North America is not searching for just the right church. For some, accepting this reality is difficult. For others, naming it and going with this recognition is liberating – discovering a way to understand the reality in which they find themselves.

This new reality became clear as our family watched "our show." Somehow, we were drawn into the television show *Survivor* when it began and we have remained Jeff Probst fans ever since. Each season we watch religiously, cheering our favorites toward the goal of Sole Survivor. One night when our television cable service was interrupted, we had to wait to the next day, watching on AT&T U-verse. Yes, the episode was a day late, but we could still take it in. Now AT&T U-verse also has commercials interspersed in its programming. As we watched, Ron Reagan (former president's son) came on the screen, giving a short speech. He advocated for the separation of church and state, speaking as a member of an association of atheists. His tone was pleasant, his message made good sense, and his manner was attractive. Then right at the end of his presentation he said, "I'm Ron Reagan, and I'm not afraid of burning in hell." We looked at one another with the looks people give meaning, "did he really say what I thought he said?" Our youngest daughter piped up, "I was right there with him on the separation of church and state, but with that last part...he seemed pretty angry."

Not only is the general public not looking for a church, there are plenty of people who are angry, feeling repelled by organized religion. Through various experiences some people have arrived at a place where they have at the very least written off the Church as irrelevant. Others see the Church as not only benign, but as doing great harm to people and our world. They see the massive amounts of money going into buildings and wonder how much poverty and need could be alleviated if these funds were diverted. They learn about the corruption of Church leaders, with personal and professional moral failures, and the trust level drops further. These, plus many other influences, lead plenty of people to distrust when it comes to the Church.

Ironically, while regard for the institutional church is declining, regard for the way of life taught by Jesus Christ is rising. Dan Kimball tells the story of interviewing students on the University of California at Santa Cruz campus. He and a small crew filmed these brief interviews for use in their worship gathering. They asked random students two questions:

1. What comes to mind when you hear the name Jesus?
2. What comes to mind when you hear the word Christian?

Answers to question number one were delightful to our Christian ears:

"Jesus was beautiful."

"I want to be like Jesus."

"Jesus was a liberator of women."

"I want to be a follower of Jesus."

"Jesus was enlightened and had higher truth."

Answers to the second question were disturbing:

"Christians have taken the teachings of Jesus and really messed them up."

"I want to be a Christian, but I have never met one."

"Christians are dogmatic and closed-minded."

"Christians are supposed to be loving, but I've never met any who are."

"Christians should be taken outside and shot."

Kimball shares further that only one out of sixteen interviewed even claimed to know a Christian. What they knew came from hearsay and general observations in the larger culture. What they knew of Jesus, they liked and respected, while the reverse was true when it comes to Christians.[7]

There continues to be this great hunger in humanity for connection with the divine. This has been, and continues onward, for we human beings. Yet, our culture is disillusioned with the Church, or even hostile. It's time to detangle ourselves from the Modern Era church expression, giving ourselves permission to discover a new expression of God's Church which is more relevant to our times.

What then does this mean?

Just like the Attractional Church is driven by one primary assumption with auxiliary corollaries, so goes the Missional Church.

Primary Assumption of the Missional Church – God is on mission in the world, unveiling the kingdom, while reconciling and healing the world.

Upon first exposure, most Christ-followers quickly agree with this assumption. In fact, most don't see any conflict with the assumption driving the Attractional church model. When we begin to consider what this primary assumption means, then the differences grow clear. These corollary assumptions help clarify.

God's mission is not to save your church

This is often the request behind the stated request. When we are called to consult with congregations, they don't state their request as, "Please help us save our church!" But when we listen carefully, this is often their unstated concern.

And, wouldn't you feel the same way if your congregation was facing its demise? Christ-followers in these congregations carry many deep life-giving experiences in their hearts as a result of being part of this congregation's life. Now they want their children or grandchildren to have similar faith experiences with this particular faith community. The desire to pass on a healthy faith legacy to the next generation is strong, and is often expressed through wanting one's church to survive and thrive. These are natural and healthy motives.

While this desire for one's church to survive and thrive is so real and poignant that it hurts, and while we might carry great empathy for those in these congregations, we also must ask ourselves, "Is saving our church also God's goal?" Missional theology moves our focus beyond ourselves to the larger canvas of God's movement. God is on mission in the world, unveiling the kingdom while healing and reconciling. Whether a particular local faith community resonates with God's mission and joins it is another question. As harsh as it sounds, it is helpful when a church can move beyond itself and realize that God's primary mission is in the world. God's primary mission is not to save any particular local church.

The degree to which your church joins God on mission is the degree to which your church will be saved.
Before we launch into application, clarification on wording is needed here. What do we mean through the use of this word, "saved?" Here we do not mean institutional survival or revitalization. The Missional Church Movement is not a back-door way to revitalize your congregation, for the purpose of ensuring longevity and institutional renewal. The Missional Church Movement is not the next best church growth initiative cloaked in different language. This is not sleight of hand positioning, which is actually focused on twentieth century metrics. No, salvation here refers to something far deeper than metrics and institutional strength.

"It's all about soul," to quote musician Billy Joel. When your church joins God on mission in the world, then your church resonates with its deepest calling. Salvation then, for a congregation, is found in aligning itself with God's mission. The degree to which your congregation can join God on mission, is the degree to which your congregation will find itself immersed in the movement of God in the world. This will breathe life into your congregation's spirit. Joining God on mission helps your church find its soul.

Now, does this also mean your congregation's institutional concerns will be resolved? Perhaps and perhaps not. God's mission is in the world, with the church as an instrument of this mission. The more your congregation is involved with God's mission, the better. But better does not mean more money or members. Better means more spirit and congruent focus. As your congregation finds its spirit again through joining God on mission, it may become more attractive to others who want to join you. While at the very same time, it may be that no one notices this shift in your focus. The goal here is not institutional revitalization in terms of buildings, bodies, and budgets. The goal is to live out one's calling as fully and effectively as possible. The institutional effects of this alignment are unpredictable. Yet, wouldn't you rather be aligned with God's mission, living out your calling as a congregation, regardless of what's in it for you?

Your church's salvation is in giving itself away (not in protecting itself or focusing on survival).
I'm remembering one consultation conversation with a lay leadership team wherein the discussion went on and on. Weariness and frustration were growing as the group continued to generate ideas about how to attract newcomers to their congregation. This agenda was not the stated agenda, but since it was present behind the overt agenda for our work, it surfaced. After their frustration reached significant levels, I found myself saying what everyone in the room already knew. "I hate to tell you, or to state the obvious, but there really are not people out there who are eager to join you in order to help you pay the light bill." The initial response included nervous laughter, followed by substantive conversation about focus and priorities. This group of lay leaders knew this before it was spoken. They knew that their church's ability to meet its financial obligations along with other institutional concerns, is a non-issue for those in their community. There really aren't people in their community who want to join them to help address their institutional concerns. They were relieved someone finally said out loud what they knew intuitively. This is the time to shift the conversation, to shift our focus, to the

first clause in the statement above.

Your church's salvation is in giving itself away. We find Jesus using so many analogies about the calling of his disciples in the New Testament. Grain falling to the ground and dying, giving up control over our priorities and following Christ, embracing our brokenness before finding healing...dying to self appears to be the default way of salvation (finding genuine life on earth). This is the calling of God's church. Communities of faith are called to avoid self-centered and self-aggrandizing behavior. We are called to give ourselves away in service, joining God on mission in the world. When we do so, we discover life. We gain a foretaste of what life will be like when God's kingdom comes fully on this earth, like it is in heaven.

Letting Go

"This is a time for a dramatically new vision. The current predicament of churches in North America requires more than mere tinkering with long-assumed notions about identity and mission of the church. Instead, as many knowledgeable observers have noted, there is a need for reinventing or rediscovering the church in this new kind of world."[8]

George Hunsberger

Perceptive readers who are involved in church-as-we've-known-it, quickly recognize most congregations are not designed to implement missional theology. Most have a missions committee, which leads the church to do mission work, as one part of their congregation's ministries. Becoming a missional church though requires a huge leap in understanding, acceptance, and practice. We are to the acceptance phase now. What must we accept in

order to move further along the missional pathway? What must
we let go in order to take hold of new ways of being church?

*We must accept that church- as-we-have-known-it is not
returning, letting go of our expectations that it will return, along
with our actions designed to bring it back.* Letting go is difficult,
especially when what we are losing is dear to us. To those who
have been a part of the Christian movement for some time,
letting go of the ways we have been church can be heart-
wrenching. These faith practices and approaches to being church
have formed and shaped our lives. Believing they have run their
course and new ways of being church are needed involves quite a
faith makeover.

But many of us are there. Many have tried over and over to do
what used to work...better, with more vigor, with nuanced
change. Yet, the inevitable result of putting more effort into an
outdated church paradigm is frustration. The harder we work,
with lesser results than we expect, the quicker we reach crisis
stage. That's when we grow more open to change; when we are
convinced our previous church model is no longer sufficient for
partnering with God on mission.

We hear and see this struggle between paradigms regularly in
churches. I remember one older gentleman involved in a
consultation process. During the conversation about their church
he described his struggle this way, "We raised our family here,
and now my grandkids are here. We had so many significant, life-
giving experiences in this church (pausing while tearing up)....I
want this church to continue to do those same activities so that
my grandchildren can have those same experiences. At the same
time, through this exploration we are doing, I'm becoming aware

that if we continue doing church as we have, my grandchildren may not stay around to experience it. I guess I need to be open to change and following the Spirit's lead."

What a poignant confession of the struggle for many Christ-followers...letting go is necessary in order to take hold of the new. This gentleman is on the way to embracing a new reality, motivated by his love for God, his children, and grandchildren. Letting go of church-as-we-have-known-it involves changing our expectations. Then we also lay aside our efforts to reinvigorate a worn-out church paradigm.

We must accept our context for what it is, letting go of anger or bitterness directed toward our society and culture. The gentleman described above is realizing the cultural assumptions which guided his generation in their church life are no longer at play. New cultural assumptions are operational, guiding the formation and development of organizations and movements of all kinds. Some Christ-followers are collecting their angst about this, hoarding and secretly nurturing it, while it slowly poisons their souls. They don't mean to, but they are so hurt by church-as-we-have-known-it passing away that they become angry and bitter. Perhaps this is a phase people experiencing loss must move through, but it is certainly not a life-giving way to live long term. Harboring anger and bitterness never leads to positive outcomes.

When people do not address and resolve their strong emotions related to loss in healthy ways, they tend to act them out. Unfortunately, in the community of faith context, this usually presents itself as judgment. "If this younger generation was just more committed, then we wouldn't have this problem in church." How many variations of this statement have we heard by now? As one might expect, when a congregation adopts this perspective, they run off the very people they would like to include. Judgment is not the work of Christian disciples.

During Shift presentations I enjoy using a video which comes out each year on YouTube called "Did You Know?" Participants are presented example after example of how quickly the world is changing. Change itself is not new, having been around forever. The pace of change is what's different. Students working on a four-year technical degree find that what they learned in year one is outdated by year three. Is it any wonder that processes, structures, and methods we employed for being church twenty years ago serve as impediments to fruitful ministry now?

We must accept the church is facing adaptive challenges just like all other organizations and institutions in our society, releasing the desire to enshrine one way of being church. We live in a swirl of change. People know it and experience it daily. Sometimes it's overwhelming, resulting in the thought, "doesn't anything stay the same anymore?" Then one considers God. Extrapolating from the common belief that God doesn't change, one gets the idea that God's Church should not change. It's a small leap from the steadfastness and faithfulness of God (experienced as stability) to viewing the Church in a similar manner. Since the Church is representative of God in some ways, then shouldn't the Church also be immune to shifts in time and culture? This kind of thinking results in faith community islands in a sea of change with ever diminishing dry land available to them.

Peter Senge was a prophet (no, not in the faith-based Biblical sense). He was a prophet in that he saw a likely future ahead of time. *The Fifth Discipline*, written in 1990, was a groundbreaking book about becoming an effective organization or corporation in a shifting environment. Senge suggested that healthy and sustained organizations invest themselves in significant learning. In fact, he predicted that the organizations and corporations who survived and thrived in the future were those who could learn the fastest. "Learning Organizations," became Senge's name for those who learn quickly and adapt.[9] Now, we might call this Adaptive Theory. Those groups of people who learn what's needed and then adjust themselves to their current context will continue to exist, as well as discover new and effective ways of being in their culture.

Since this reality is so apparent, what holds churches back from viewing themselves as learning organizations with the need to adapt? Some congregations believe that faith is enough. When we just trust God and remain faithful (code language for continuing to do what we've always done), then we will harvest the results for which we are looking. Typically this statement is made when congregations are feeling overwhelmed, throwing up their hands in the face of their adaptive challenges.

Accepting the perspectives identified above is part of the letting go, or winnowing process. We are shedding understandings, perspectives, and attitudes which no longer help us move forward. Though there is pain and grief in this process, it's not unrecognizable. Letting go and taking hold is the process of salvation. We die to self, are buried with Christ (baptism) and then are raised again to new life. We stop clinging, clutching, and controlling life...releasing our wills to God's will. When we become like the proverbial grain of wheat, falling to the ground, we discover resurrection.

Then we move from this attractional church question, "How do

we attract more people to what we are doing?"
To this missional church question, "What is God doing in our community, and how do we need to change to join God on mission?

CHAPTER TEN
MAKING THE SHIFT TOWARD
THE MISSIONAL CHURCH

As a congregation moves toward missional, spiritual vigor is needed. This is when the Disciple Developing Movement and the Missional Church Movement need each other. When the Missional Church Movement began, few authors and proponents mentioned the need for invigorated faith and spiritual vigor. They tended to assume that churches were already engaged in sufficient discipleship processes, with disciples ready to move forward to join God on mission in the world. Perhaps this is my greatest critique of the Missional Church Movement; assuming the current level of disciple development in congregations is sufficient. I don't want to be unfair to Missional Church theorists and practitioners; it just seems that developing disciples is off their radar screens and not their focus.

I'm happy for the opportunity in this book to lay these two movements out, side by side (we will include the third movement later). They need one another. In fact, they are in a reciprocally reinforcing relationship. Congregations who launch their Missional Church Movement without sufficient spiritual invigoration or refueling opportunities will run dry. Though their activity and action is in itself spiritually invigorating, the soul needs nurtured in many ways besides meaningful action. Simultaneously, congregations who launch their Disciple Development Movement without sufficient opportunity for engaging the world around them, will experience a diminished spirituality (too self-focused). Disciple Development and Missional Engagement are the yen and yang of faith. They are a complimentary couple who support each other as well as challenge one another to avoid falling into myopic ways of being church.

We have explored the theology of the missional church movement, followed by identifying its primary assumption, along with corollaries. Our awareness is rising, bringing insights into a different way of perceiving God and God's mission. As progress is being made, the journey continues. Gaining insight and awareness does not necessarily lead to behavior change (learning theory again). Learning is stimulating, yet continuing the developmental journey is our calling; to live our faith. Now it's time to take hold of new missional practices, launching a Missional Movement in our congregations, joining God on mission more fully.

Making The Shift
Check your motivation
Before launching your boat into the missional stream, consider what you are transporting. The most common mistake made in reference to the missional church movement is believing this is a sly and subtle way to grow our churches. Yes, we agree that we are called to join God on mission in the world, but isn't there something really good in this for our church? Won't this ultimately lead to greater numbers and institutional strength?

Isn't the missional church movement simply the next best way to do evangelism, while not really appearing to do so, becoming more culturally relevant?

Evangelism may be a part of being missional. Yet, joining God on mission in the world is a far larger activity. David Bosch is a South African missiologist who is credited with helping initiate the missional church movement. Others, like Australian Michael Frost have nurtured this movement along, basing their understanding on the work of Bosch. Listen how Frost describes his understanding of the missional church as larger than evangelism or church growth.

> *"David Bosch, the South African missiologist whose work first set me and many others on this missional journey, once wrote, 'Mission is more and different than recruitment to our brand of religion; it is the alerting people to the universal reign of God through Christ.'[1] And with that he said a mouthful. To reduce mission to the recruitment of new church members is like turning an ox into a bouillon cube. Rather, mission is the most extraordinary cosmic/global activity of 'alerting people to the universal reign of God through Christ.'"[2]*

Risking redundancy, it's worth repeating....the purpose of becoming missional is not to attract more people to our congregations. The missional church movement is really not about us. It is about God, and God's mission of healing and reconciliation in the world.

Again, Frost helps make this completely clear. *"And when church leaders read evangelism as a chiefly come-to-us activity, they end*

up thinking that being missional is just the latest way of being
uber-attractional. Yet the truly missional energy of the church
flows outward as an incarnational impulse."[3]

As your congregation engages this missional church movement,
coming back to the purpose of your efforts repeatedly is part of
the process. We human beings drift toward self-focus. Given this,
we can expect ourselves to constantly be considering what's in it
for us; for our congregation. When our answer is, "An opportunity
to give ourselves to God's mission, giving ourselves away through
service in God's vineyard," then we know our motivation is more
faithful. When we can give ourselves over to God's mission
without regard for what's in it for our organization, then we are
moving in the right direction.

Check your spirituality
Before you launch, remember that God is already there. Our goal
is to join God on mission in the world. This means that God is on
mission in the world already. So as you go, you will discover the
kingdom of God happening before your eyes. Healing,
peacemaking, reconciliation, justice, salvation....these are
happening all around us all the time, when we have the eyes to
see and ears to hear. Given this, we are not God's greatest gift to
the world. We are simply part of God's movement in the world.
Our initial activity is to wake up to what God is doing around us.

Given this, there are three spiritually based qualities we will need
within us. Humility is first. It's time to dismount the spiritual high
horse and recognize our rightful place in God's kingdom. We are
instruments of God's grace and peace, yes...just like are so many
other people in this world – some who don't even know it. Our
calling is first to humbly look for God's activity, wherever and

however it may be showing up, and then join God in that activity. This requires humble Christ-followers, who have no self-perception as "better than" or superior to the "others" out there. Spiritually superior attitudes are apparent so quickly to people, functioning like spiritual repellent. Humility is necessary to join God in the world, rather than to believe we have the corner on God's activity.

Respect closely follows, and even mirrors, humility. My calling has morphed and changed in its expression in many ways over time, allowing me to serve in a variety of ways. Becoming a therapist is part of my journey. There is a vigorous and substantial supervision process beyond graduate school required to work as a professional counselor. Presenting cases to an experienced and qualified supervisor and supervision group is part of the licensure process. I remember one case I was presenting wherein I was struggling to help my clients, wanting input from this wiser supervisor. The input I received was not what I expected. "Mark, before you can help any client, you have to find something you respect about the client. If you don't respect anything, the client will know it, and won't be able to hear a thing you say." This wisdom drove me to my faith. At the very least, I can respect that every person is created in the image of God. Everyone has something of God's imprint within him or herself. We are all God's children, seen in this way. I can respect that. While joining God on mission in the world, prepare yourself to take respect to whomsoever you will meet.

Receptivity is the third spiritual practice we will need. Yes we are Christ-followers, vessels of God's grace and instruments of God's peace. Yet we are also looking for how God is already at work in the world around us. So as we engage the world around us, we must be open to learning; to being taught by those we encounter. Listening, learning, engaging...this is where we begin. We avoid beginning with telling, teaching, or recommending. We must be open to the idea that we will be changed through engagement with the world. We will shift, learn, grow, and even be transformed. Life is about giving and receiving. We go forward with receptivity, being genuinely open to those we meet. The Missional Church Movement is not about pretending to like others so that then we can correct them for being less than they should be. Humility, respect, and receptivity are spiritually based attitudes and practices which will serve us well on the missional journey.

Embrace Missional Theology and Language
I'm serving as the interim pastor and consultant in a First Baptist Church. This church community is full of faithful, loving, good-hearted people. They intentionally called me to this interim role, knowing they had significant lingering issues and challenging obstacles to address. This ministry is fascinating, mixing-it-up around life and faith. The two questions we are engaging are about being disciples and then being a community of Christ-followers. I'm finding this faith community to be exceptionally open to rethinking what it means to be church. Part of their openness comes from the painful conflict preceding our coming together; one which resulted in the exodus of a large group. The pain of this experience drives this church its knees. In addition, this church also includes some mature Christ-followers who have sensed the world is different, knowing that church-as-we-have-known-it no longer resonates within their context. They are open to new concepts, theological viewpoints, and methodology.

The result of their willingness to explore, learn, and adapt is a new vision. Here is how First Baptist is articulating their vision statement: *First Baptist Church will engage a three-year transformation process, becoming a disciple-developing missional church.* Through reading this book, you have a sense of how transformative this vision can be for a traditional kind of church. Admittedly, some disciples in this church are more on board with this approach than others. Some still believe this is a great way to put bodies in the pews and money in the offering plate. Yet others are intrigued with the possibility of focusing on what's been in their spiritual dreams for years.

In listening to them, I'm noticing shifts in the dialogue. Some are subtle, while other shifts are very direct and intentional. Before this disciple-developing missional church movement began, their questions were:

"How do we get more young people into this church?"
"How can we recover those who left during the conflict, or even those who drifted away over the last fifteen years?"
"Who will volunteer to staff a youth and children's ministry here?"
"How do we need to change our worship service to be more relevant?"
"How can we attract more people so that our budget will expand, helping us call the pastors and staff we need?"

Now, I hear fewer of these questions. The conversation is moving. Yes, it is still a work in progress, yet the questions and statements I hear are different:

"What are people in our community talking about; focused on? And how can we be part of that dialogue?"
"How can we get beyond ourselves? We are tired of

always thinking about what we need as a church."
"How can we support each other more, since living this
disciple life is really challenging?"
"We are ready to do something; we are tired of being
passive Christians."

These are subtle, yet dramatic shifts. Making the shift to missional
includes engaging missional theology and learning new language.
This is the movement from seeing church as about us, to seeing
church as joining God's mission in the world. This shift changes
everything. As people engage this new (yet ancient)
understanding of God and God's mission, their language shifts.

To support this movement, pastors, church staff, and lay leaders
can intentionally shift their language. Engaging learning
experiences around this book or other resources, will help shape
the theology and language of everyone in the congregation.
Leaders can lead by intentionally speaking this new language,
knowing that language forms us.

Identifying your missional engagement strategy
In some ways this appears counter to what you just read about
spirituality. Can one have a strategy and be truly open to what
happens in the moment? Yes and no. One cannot if this strategy
objectifies people, making them objects in our plan. A strategy is
helpful when it gives us guidance on how to grow ourselves in
relation to others. Our missional strategy gives guidance on what
to do with what we learn as we engage the world around us.

Leslie Newbigin made great contributions to our understanding of
being missional people. Too many theologians and practitioners
to list have described his work, taking cues from him on how to

engage our world missionally. Newbigin left England, serving as a missionary in India. When he returned to England in 1974, he didn't recognize the religious landscape, having moved from a Christian culture to a largely secular society. Taking note of this big shift, Newbigin brought what he learned in India to his home culture, the eyes of a missionary.

Alan Roxburgh and M. Scott Boren use the image of a triangle to describe Newbigin's strategy.[4]

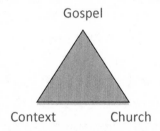

Gospel

Context   Church

Our typical way of engaging the world is to first identify the mission of the church, followed by engaging the gospel. Then we move to our context, trying to build bridges of relevance between the church and its context. Newbigin challenged us to reverse this order. Effective missionaries begin with their context, listening and learning, bringing what is learned back to the gospel. What does the gospel have to do with our context? After this dialogue happens, that's when Newbigin suggests we move toward shaping the church. The way we are church is formed first through the interaction between the context and gospel, giving shape to how we express church.

This informs and shapes our missional strategy. Our missional strategy gives us guidance, while not objectifying others. We begin with where we are, our context, asking where God is active in this world. We engage with the people, organizations, and structures in our community – learning as much as we can while building relationships and connections. Then we engage the gospel, and the scriptures, examining how these interact with each other. Structuring and organizing the church comes last, informed and shaped by this rich dialogue between our context and the gospel.

Alan Roxburgh uses Newbigin's triangle above for helping us visualize this three-way on-going conversation between community, gospel, and church. One phrase I would insert into this strategizing is "Holy Experimenting."

Who among us knows the mind of God? Who can perfectly discern God's calling for a faith community? On the one hand, God is beyond our knowing; is mystery. So we don't claim a perfect understanding of God's will or intention for our personal or communal lives. At the same time, we do believe that God provides the guidance we need in order to follow. It's like God leaves bread crumbs sprinkled through the woods, providing the path for us to follow. Or some would say that God gives the macro call; to follow and partner with God around the kingdom coming to earth. Then God leaves the micro calls; working out the details, to us, after giving us the gifts and talents to make progress. However this happens, we are called to partner with God in the kingdom's appearance on earth. Holy Experimenting is one way we discover what the kingdom looks like and how to engage with it more fully.

What then does this "Holy Experimenting" phrase mean? First we engage our context, our community, with open and receptive ears, eyes, hearts, and minds. We hope to learn where God is active in this community. We want to meet people, learn from them, and strengthen relationships and connections. We are eager to recognize assets and strengths, as well as seeing the brokenness. Then we take this learning to the gospel. We ask what the good news of Christ has to do with what we learn in and from our community. Where do the gospel and what we see in our community align? Then we move to considering what we might do as a congregation. This is when we engage in holy experimenting. When we are holy experimenting,

- We engage in activities without knowing the outcome beforehand
- We are making our best guesses about what might contribute to God's kingdom
- We recognize and accept that experiments may lead to any number of outcomes, each a step forward
- We continue our "learner's attitude," staying open to God's intervention as we go along
- We discover unforeseen new missional pathways, given our experimentation orientation
- We are able to pivot quickly, updating our action-plan as we move along
- We give ourselves freedom to try many new missional engagement actions without over-burdening them with expectations of "success"

I'm reading an excellent book filled with spiritual guidance by Brian McLaren, *We Make The Road By Walking*.[5] The book title is not original, often used to describe life's journey. McLaren makes the case for discovering a new way of life by moving ahead; by standing up and moving forward in trust and faith. God's guidance often occurs as we are moving forward, rather than before our first steps. This is what holy experimenting is about. We learn from our community, we engage the gospel, and then launch out into missional engagement. Course corrections will happen as we move forward. We will encounter dead end streets, having to back up and make another turn. We will find beautiful vistas which expand our spirits and enliven our hearts. We will discover what life in the kingdom of God is about. Holy experimenting is a perspective and attitude which allows us to make the road by walking.

All this experimentation talk sounds risky....and it is, when we cling to the idea that we must know where we are going before we start the journey. When we look at the Biblical story, there were few calls which included descriptions of the final destination within the initial call. Perhaps Abraham and Sarai are the most notable in this regard. "Get up and go to a land which you know not of." Hans Kung reinforces the recognition that we are a sent people rather than a settled Church. *"A church which pitches its tents without constantly looking out for new horizons, which does not continually strike camp, is being untrue to its calling. ...(We must) lay down our longing for certainty, accept what is risky, and live by improvisation and experiment."*[6]

Feed your faith community missional engagement stories
For those who have been a part of the Christian movement for a long time, you may recognize this ancient word: "testimonies." I can remember deep in Appalachia those fascinating services wherein the agenda was to allow whoever was so moved to stand up and testify to what God is doing in his/her life. Often great emotion accompanied the testifying, providing for moving and sometimes even scary worship services.

Though the word testimonies fell from grace in our common language, story telling still resonates with us as a powerful way to express our faith journeys. Your missional engagement strategy needs a communication feedback loop. After engaging the community with an eye toward learning and connection, then you are ready to share what you are learning and experiencing. This is a great time for disciples to address the larger church, typically during worship. Some may choose other forms of communication, like newsletters, email blasts, Facebook, etc. The point is that sharing our missional engagement stories energizes those who hear. We vicariously experience missional engagement, warming our hearts and encouraging our doing. We are far more likely to join the missional movement when we hear another disciple telling his/her story than when we only hear missional engagement described. Look for every opportunity possible to tell stories about how your intention is happening, how missional engagement is taking shape.

PART FOUR
CONSUMER CULTURE TO
SACRED PARTNERING

"...the ultimate heresy: that we can be religious in isolation from one another,"

Robin R. Meyers[1]

Through personal experience, I am very clear on two truths about my desire to live in the Way of Jesus. These are not highly sophisticated theological arguments or insights. Instead, they are truth to me; learned the hard way.

First, I cannot do it alone.
I've tried. I've tried living in the Way of Jesus, whether anyone else wants to go with me. The result...epic fail. Sure, I can live the cultural Christianity I've learned through years of being immersed in church culture. Yet, I cannot sustain robust engagement in living out the teachings and lifestyle to which Christ calls by myself. It's too hard to do and sustain alone.

Appendix 3 – Blog Post: Just Me And Jesus Will Do Fine

Second, when I am in relationship with partners intent on living in the Way of Jesus, I am more able to sustain Christ-following. Experience has and is teaching me this truth. When we covenant together around shifting our lifestyles, offering mutual support and encouragement, then I make progress. When I am challenged by people who love me and are in relationship with me, then I tend to rise to the challenge. When I know these people expect the best from me, I tend to live toward their expectations. When I share a sorrow with my partners, then it becomes a half-sorrow. When I'm in faith-based partnership relationships, I am much more of a disciple of Jesus Christ.

God designed it this way. Since we are social creatures made for relationship, God provided for this need. The Church is designed to provide a community of faith with whom we can "work out our salvation." Being in relationship with other Christ-followers whose goal is to be conformed to the image of Christ, makes living in the Way of Jesus far more possible.

These three big moves for the 21st century Church are in sequential order. When intentionally living in the Way of Jesus, we are quickly sensitized to our inability to go it alone. Just try it. Try drinking deeply from the well of Christ's teachings followed by integration into your life while isolated from a faith community. Very quickly you will discover your inability to sustain this way of living by yourself. In fact, living as Jesus taught is so challenging that some of the early church fathers taught that the Sermon on the Mount is intentionally impossible to actually live. They believed Jesus gave this teaching to sensitize us to our flawed human condition, driving us to rely on the grace of God.

Certainly that is the experience of many of us – the realization that we cannot live fully into Jesus' description of this Godly way of living. At the same time, it seems that Jesus DID intend for us to embody his teachings. These teachings are given as the Rule of Life so to speak for those who would participate with God in world transformation. Though none of us will be perfect in our discipleship, all of us are called to apply ourselves to living as disciples. We are all called to become the change we want to see in the world, joining God's mission to transform this world. To this end, we need sacred partners, a community of faith, with whom to travel.

This movement, consumer culture to sacred partnering, is no small shift. What's at stake is the very nature, or essence, of the Church. When it comes to our Postmodern understanding of the Church, the stakes could not be any higher. The very nature of God's Church is what we are considering. First, let's trace how we arrived where we are. What makes this a pertinent discussion now? What is it about our Postmodern world that the word "consumer" is even associated with our understanding of church life?

CHAPTER ELEVEN
DEMISE OF CONSUMER CHURCH CULTURE

Influences of Consumer Culture - How did we get here?
The Church has this on-going love/hate relationship with culture. Culture influences nearly every aspect of who we are as people at any point in time. Simultaneously, Christ-followers live in culture while not being defined by culture. We are called to be defined by our relationship with God, living in the Way of Jesus. So although we believe we are separate and distinct from the larger culture around us, we can look back at church history, observing how directly the Church has been shaped and influenced by its cultural context. The same is true for church-as-we-know-it now. These three particular cultural themes below directly influenced the 20th century Church to become what it is.

Almighty Market-Mentality
Intelligent church leaders recognize the reality that market forces are the river in which North American organizations swim. To survive, and especially to thrive, is to accept and adapt in the context wherein one finds oneself. Some very intelligent church leaders believe market forces are inescapable, giving themselves and their church models over to them.

I had to do a double-take when I learned about this particular church's marketing scheme. They identified a Sunday worship service, during which a drawing would take place. One lucky worshipper present that day would walk away with a brand new Jeep Grand Cherokee. They were giving away a really nice SUV; brand new, with all the bells and whistles. I considered taking a vacation day from my interim pastor responsibilities; getting myself to that church for the drawing. We could use another car at the time. This church recognizes the consumer culture in which they live, believing their job is to attract people to what they are doing, thereby producing results. Their attendance that day was huge.

Many of us laugh at such obvious marketing ploys, yet most churches engage in marketing at some level. How many congregations have hired a "marketing professional" to help them brand their church, developing an appealing logo supported with a nice website? Most of us recognize what market-driven organizations in our culture must do to survive and thrive. Missional Church expert Darrell Guder identifies our tendencies.

> *"This model (market-driven church) has a ring of truth about it. It describes only too well assumptions about membership, programs, structure, success, and purpose that give shape to today's church culture, 'the way we do things around here.' It certainly illumines the current circumstance in which the churches live, a pervasive religious consumerism driven by the quest to meet personally defined religious needs. It also explains the heavy concentration of church efforts to produce and promote programs, and it corresponds with the emphasis in one stream of literature flowing out of the church*

growth movement. That stream has accepted the commercial image without question by commending strategies for effectively and successfully 'marketing your church.'"[1]

I (along with others) believe that part of the demise of Christendom as we know it in Western culture is directly tied to the sublimation of the gospel to consumerism. We have bowed down to the idol of the free market paradigm, shaping the Beloved Community to look like other organizations in our environment. We describe our people as church members, but other words would suffice just fine: clients, customers, constituents. How much does it alarm us that these consumer-oriented words can serve the same function as the phrase "church members?" Walter Brueggemann describes it well, *"The contemporary American church is so acculturated to the American ethos of consumerism that is has little power to believe or act."[2]* Missioner Michael Frost views this almighty-market mentality similarly. *"My point, rather, is to suggest that the church's very understanding of its purpose and mission is often shaped more obviously by the free market than by the teaching of Jesus."[3]* When we combine the attractional church model with an almighty market mentality, then we do everything we can to connect with potential clients or religious consumers. This can be done. We can figure out how to gather a crowd in our sanctuary. But might we lose our souls in the process?

Consumer Culture Shapes Our Language
At how many grocery stores do you shop? Our family makes purchases at five grocery stores during most two-week periods. How do we decide where to shop? The criteria we use includes: proximity, bargains, quality of particular items, specialty items,

organic food considerations, etc.

We are grateful for so many choices when it comes to our food needs and preferences. This makes us consumers in the eyes of grocery stores; and in our own eyes. Consumers are those who survey the options before themselves, then making purchasing decisions based on conscious or unconscious criteria. This is what it means to be a consumer of goods and services.

The United States of America, as well as many other countries around the world, are obviously free market economies. We are consumers of goods and services in this free market economy. Many of us live in communities which offer many choices when it comes to how we meet our needs and wants. Through this pervasive understanding of ourselves as consumers, we develop a consumer identity. Certainly we are more than consumers, yet consumer becomes part of who we are.

Just like we are moving from member identity to disciple identity, so we need language changes for describing the move from consumer culture to sacred partnering. Consumer-oriented churches call their participants members or volunteers. We are members of organizations. When it comes to being part of this living organism called the Church, we are disciples. But how do we describe the relationship of these disciples to each other and to their church?

Just think for a moment about the phrases we use to describe our church experience:

- We go to church
- We go to worship

- We go to church to be spiritually fed

We can see the consumer perspective running through all these statements.

One of the greatest concerns we hear from church leaders is around volunteer recruitment. People don't want to commit to a three-year term on the lay leadership team, or the heavy investment required for member-care ministry, or even six-months of teaching a Sunday School class. Those who see themselves as volunteers recognize that volunteering is optional. Disciples serve. Serving is a natural part of living as a disciple.

Organism To Organization – We become what we measure
It's such a basic discussion. We engaged it in seminary and it rises up frequently with church professionals. Is the Church an organism or an organization? The realistic among us typically answer, "yes." The Church is an organism which has to function like an organization to be sustained in our market-driven cultural environment.

This appears to be a fairly insignificant discussion. Yet, a huge danger lurks in perspective. What the Church in America has done is recognize its environmental setting and adapt. Isn't this what all successful living organisms do? Those who adapt survive, with the opportunity to thrive. Those who do not adapt become extinct.

So, the Church in North America largely appears to be an organization. It is similar to non-profit organizations, structured with paid professionals and volunteer boards to guide the organization. Volunteer management, participant recruitment, and staffing on tight budgets are major activities of these churches, as they are in other non-profit organizations. Many churches develop strategic ministry plans, modeled after the business plan of for-profit organizations and strategic plans of NPOs. When consultants become adept at strategic planning in NPOs, they are able to make the small step to strategic planning with churches.

In teaching about churches, I'm not alone in describing churches as a group of people who function like an organization. At the same time, when the layers of the organization are peeled back, the beating heart of an organism is underneath. At its center, the church is a living, breathing organism with a living pulse. This is how we have explained the nature of the church in our context: an organization which is an organism at its core.

The following two insights shape any group of people:
1. We become what we measure
2. To what the leaders tend, becomes reality over time

We didn't mean for this to happen. Call it mission-creep or the slow subtle slide into institutionalism. Whatever we call it, this principle of people groups has become crystal clear for churches. We become what we measure. When evaluating how well we are doing as a church, most church members will first look to the statistics about membership, funding, and physical plant. These are the most obvious and most easily measured aspects of church life. These measures are very similar to how other organizations in our culture evaluate themselves. Of course we tell ourselves these are only tools to help the deeper, more significant mission to happen. But over time, our intent becomes lost in our practice. What we measure becomes our reality.

Similarly, what the leaders in congregations focus on, talk about, and lift up shapes our understanding of our purpose. Lay and professional leaders in congregations of most any denomination could be transported to another church of any other denomination and follow the flow of the board meeting easily. Reading of the minutes, examining the previous month's financial picture with the Treasurer's report, followed by committee reports, completing old business, and entertaining new business will pretty much complete the agenda. The vast majority of board meetings are focused on organizational measures. Of course they begin with a devotional, to set a spiritual tone...while participants chafe at the delay in getting down to business.

The focus of leaders tends to become the priorities of the organization over time. Leaders, ordained and lay, who focus on organizational measures, train others to believe this is what is important. Sure, we know they are only organizational measures of deeper realities, yet our behavior does not confirm this awareness. We behave as if this is a business or institution, just like others in our cultural environment. The result is that we train ourselves, adapt the church, to behave just like other organizations. Over time, this becomes our reality.

Besides, who knows how to measure things like robust faith, increased spirit, loving neighbors, and bringing justice and mercy? We find it far easier to import structures, processes, and procedures from other organizations to the church rather than creatively identify what will support and advance our actual values and goals.

Results of Consumer Culture's Infiltration Into The Church
So is it any wonder that 21st century, Postmodern pilgrims bring

our consumer identity to our church community experience? We are so conditioned to see our identity in our culture as consumer that we naturally import this view to our church experience. It's not surprising this happens. Instead, we would be surprised if this did not happen.

The church then is viewed as the dispenser or provider of religious goods and services. I'm not the first (nor the last) to use this phrase for describing 21st century church culture (previous diagram). "Church Shopping," is now an accepted phrase to describe what we do when we are on the market for a new church. Consumers shop. So that's how we describe ourselves when we are looking.

In fact, identifying the mission statement of an excellent consumer church is easy. There's no need for a strategic planning process. Here it is for you.

> *We exist to be an excellent provider of religious goods and services, resulting in contented members.*
> *De facto Mission Statement of the Consumer Church*

Of course I'm not suggesting any Christ-focused church adopt this mission statement. I am suggesting this is the *de facto* mission statement for too many churches, operating quietly behind their articulated mission statement. Practically, we are organized around this statement, reflecting its influence in most all we do.

Life In The Consumer-Focused Church
Few question the viewpoint that we live in a consumer-oriented culture. Differences of opinion rise when we consider how we as Christ-followers might relate to our cultural surroundings. The

Attractional church model is based on an acculturation model; the belief that God's church should integrate the consumer culture right into its way of being. This is one way of being church. For good or ill, every decision we make brings consequences; intended and unintended. The consequences of accommodating consumer culture in our church life are large. We can describe the observed outcomes or results when the church embraces consumer culture.

Low-Expectation Organizations
The church is one of the easiest organizations to become a part - and one of the hardest organizations to leave. In some ways, this is as it should be. God is generous with grace, accepting us as we are. In general, churches try to reflect God's gracious nature by welcoming seekers into their community with as few impediments as possible. This is a theological rationale for welcoming the stranger, practicing Christian hospitality, and it is good.

Another, often more influential, perspective when it comes to church membership is a result of our consumer understanding of church. We make many assumptions about seekers who visit our worship services for the first time. We assume they are church shopping, have many choices, are easily offended or discouraged from returning, and will decide about their return to our church very quickly. Living in this Post-Christian era, we want to include and integrate those who lean toward Christ as quickly as we can. Each person becomes very important.

Thus, often churches make their requirements for church membership very low. You won't see this in their language and their initial conversation about membership. Most churches have fairly robust language about what it means to become an active member. It's on the flip side where the low expectations arise. Mainline denominations systematize their understanding of church membership. In order to maintain one's church membership from year to year, in order to remain a member in good standing, one must.... What are your denomination's requirements? Some include expectations like making a financial contribution of some kind at some point during any particular year. Attending worship and participating in communion as least one time each year is often an expectation. Rotary Clubs I've visited have far higher expectations than this for their members.

A pastor of a sizeable church reached out to me for leadership coaching. During our first conversation this pastor described the tension in the church which drove him to initiate coaching. Part of this tension rose because this pastor, the church staff, and the lay leadership team grew concerned about their low expectations for one another and the membership at large. They investigated their denomination's requirements for maintaining one's membership, finding a very low threshold, similar to the items mentioned above. Even so, they recognized many names on their roll who had not darkened the doors in years. They identified a responsible process for contacting those missing in action through phone calls, letters, and even personal visits. After a series of contacts, they removed those who did not respond or indicated they were ready to be removed from the church roll. The backlash was immediate and strong, creating tension among families and friends. Though the people removed from the roll were not participating in any way, some were highly offended by the idea that one must participate to maintain one's membership. Reward without responsibility is one outcome of the consumer culture permeating church life. There are plenty of organizations which expect far more of us than do our churches. How did we come to this?

Shallow faith, theology, and discipleship

What does it take for people to become transformed into disciples of Jesus Christ? Surely conversion is involved, yet what then? Growing up as a minister's kid, I was privileged to know many Christian disciples who were people of deep faith. These were people whose roots grew deeply into the soil of Biblical understanding, theology, and discipleship. They served as great examples of invigorated Christian disciples. Now, I ask myself how we can help people get there. When we are so focused on keeping the members we have, we are slow to call each other toward Christian maturity. This could create discomfort, which might disrupt our attractiveness.

Fragile Interpersonal Relationships

"Birds of a feather flock together." The Church Growth movement of the 1970s and 1980s recognized the tendency of our kind to mimic this saying. People tend to gather with others of their kind. The Church Growth movement recognized this powerful sociological principle, applying it to church growth. The "homogeneous principle," as it was called, became a guiding principle for those who want to grow churches quickly. There are clear, replicable marketing practices flowing from the homogeneous principle which equip any group to attract more people like them to what they are doing. Church growth became a science; a science built on the recognition that "like seeks like."

This principle combines with other powerful drivers in consumer culture. Individualism, high mobility and transience, detachment from local community connection....these dynamics which are prevalent in North American culture partner with the homogenous principle to create fragile interpersonal relationships.

Church fellowship, or faith community connections, are grounded more by cultural dynamics than by Christian identity. Since our culture is about sameness in groups, along with much encouragement to seek the good of the individual over the common good, shallow relationships are formed. Loose interpersonal connections are the inevitable outcome. Faith community connections are more about like culture than about Christian connection.

In addition, consumer culture teaches us that it is all about us. Pleasing us is the goal of companies who want us to buy their products. So, when we adopt this mindset, we believe the purpose of the church is also to please us. This makes our interpersonal relationships in this church fragile. Inevitably, this church will let us down (since human being types are involved), leaving us disappointed. Consumer members will tolerate that once, twice, or even three times. But their patience grows thin. When consumer members realize this church is not pleasing them as they wish, then a crisis arises. Loyalty to this particular church is a low value compared to the expectation of "being fed" or pleased as a consumer of religious goods and services. Thus, one's obligation to the community of faith is tenuous. Disappointed much at all, consumer members leave for greener pastures.

Conflict Aversion
So what happens in this group (consumer culture church) when fragile interpersonal relationships combined with high emphasis on individual autonomy encounter conflict? Or, what happens

when tension rises (lower levels of conflict)? Everyone's anxiety goes up.

I was doing visioning work with a congregation recently, asking what might be God's calling for them for the next season of their life together. "If your church could only move ahead in one way over the next three years, then what would that be?" One member responded, "We need to hold onto the members we have." My heart sank. This statement captures the dynamics and nuances of consumer mentality. This member was not coming from the belief that every individual has inherent worth and is valuable in God's kingdom (a healthy belief). Instead this member was expressing fear of losing members in this post-Christian consumer-oriented culture.

When churches give into the consumer perspective, then avoiding conflict at all costs is a driving principle in their faith community. The parts of the gospel which challenge us are minimized or ignored. The discomfort which comes from following Jesus and trying to live in his Way is rarely acknowledged. Since membership is fragile, why would we risk introducing challenge? The prophetic part of our faith disappears.

But even if we choose not to go there, not to introduce or discuss or teach about the challenge to our lifestyles in the gospels, conflict happens anyway. No matter what is taught, whenever two or more are gathered together, there shall be conflict. This is the way of humanity. Consumer-focused churches tend to lose members when conflict happens, given the nature of their faith community. Thus, keeping their peace is one of the highest priorities.

Community Tourism

Ever notice how churches are communities of people, yet they are often disengaged from the actual community around them? They function like commuter churches. One can drive in to worship and then drive back out to home, much like the suburban lifestyle wherein we drive into the city for working with minimal connection to other facets of city life. Little or minimal engagement with the local community around the church campus is required or expected. This church is an island in its community.

Two consumer driven dynamics combine to influence consumer-oriented churches to live in disconnected ways from their community. First, engaging with others is messy. When we get involved with others, we lose some level of control over our lives. Our schedules are compromised and interruptions to our agendas increase. Engaging with people in community and missional engagement complicate our lives. One way churches avoid this reality is to skate along the surface of their community context. They participate in their communities just enough to receive the goods and services needed, but they don't engage in missional partnerships. This would complicate their lives too much. It's easier to drive in from the suburbs, worship, and then flee to safety. It's simpler to quickly drop food at the local food pantry than to engage people around the causes of poverty. We can maintain our control over our lives and schedules when we live as community tourists. Some churches unintentionally reinforce that lifestyle.

Second, consumer church culture teaches us that it is all about us. The subtly communicated goal of our faith is personal self-actualization; me becoming a better, more fulfilled me. When this viewpoint is embraced then engaging our community is embraced only when it contributes to my development. The focus of consumer church culture is making we church members better, which may have little to do with our community context. We can maintain distance, being community tourists, since the context is nearly irrelevant to our stated purpose.

Impatience – Immediate Gratification Expectations
"Fast food" – What a strange phrase. Fast food restaurants produce mass quantities of food, very generic in nature, and then deliver meals quickly to consumers. Why wait for things which take longer. Instant gratification is held out as possible in our consumer culture. So we naturally expect the transformation of the gospel to work in us quickly too.

C. Christopher Smith and John Pattison hold up a different vision of the church in their book, *Slow Church: Cultivating Community In the Patient Way Of Jesus* (2014)[4]. They advocate for church which rejects consumer culture, especially the speed. They invite people to the long, slow work of sanctification, through close community with each other and one's community.

Focus On Pleasing Constituency
This is the most dangerous outcome for churches who capitulate to consumer culture. When we combine all the previous outcomes listed above, this focuses our attention on pleasing our constituency. Keeping members happy becomes our unstated goal. Unfortunately, pleasing our constituents is the theme running through far too many of our decisions, activities, and programs. When we adopt the consumer culture mindset, this is the inevitable outcome. Read more about this in *"How Your Church Can Escape The Happiness Trap,"* in Appendix 3.

Consumer Fatigue and Low Brand Loyalty

Do you always buy vehicles from the same car company? Some people do, though they are a small percentage of consumers. How about when it comes to smaller purchases? Do you wear only one brand of clothes?

When one lives in a free market society with so many competing choices for one's purchasing dollar, then we grow bored with consuming the same old thing over and over. Missional practitioner Michael Frost describes how consumer fatigue plays out when it comes to church participation. *"Treated like consumers by the church, young Christians are abandoning the church in the same way they abandon any other product with which they get tired. In the same way that they used to be into MySpace or Facebook or online gaming or clubbing but outgrew them, they used to be into church but outgrew that as well. They have been completely and utterly immersed in this form of consumptive Christianity, and we shouldn't be surprised when they toss the church aside like their old, outmoded iPod."[5]*

This is what life is like in the consumer church. Though not an exhaustive or comprehensive description, we gain perspective on church-as-we-have-known-it when we look through this consumer lens. Now, people go church-shopping with an internal decision guide based on our consumer identities.

The Consumer Church Decision Guide

Since we find ourselves immersed in this consumeristic culture, we are not surprised that we bring our consumer perspectives with us to church. In addition most churches accommodate to the consumer perspective, not seeing any other realistic alternatives. When these dynamics combine, we reinforce our tendencies to look at our faith through the consumer lens. Given this, we can identify the principles consumer church culture Christians use to evaluate their relationships with church.

- My decision about community of faith choice is based on my preferences, interests, and well-being.
- I am a completely free agent regarding my community of faith commitment, just like I am regarding my relationship to every other important organization in my life. Everything is up for re-negotiation at all times, with my needs being the deciding factor.
- Concern for or obligation to others in my faith community is a lesser value than my individual freedom to choose.
- Church is similar to other organizations to which I belong, participating or not participating depending on how the church meets my needs and fits with my personal lifestyle.
- I have been subtly conditioned to believe that the church is there to make me happy, so when it does not, then it means this church is failing and I should find another.

I make it a practice to ask newcomers in churches what brought them to this particular church. Typically, these principles lurk behind their answers. Savvy pastors, staff, and leaders recognize the reality of church shopping; recognizing that church shopping is a very self-focused activity. Since this is part of our cultural context, many church leaders then organize their churches in reference to this guide. The result is the Attractional Church way of being church.

Remember the consumer church's mission statement: *We exist to be an excellent provider of religious goods and services, resulting in happy and content members.* This means the goal of the consumer church is to be as attractive as possible to outsiders, while keeping the members who are currently part of the church. Therefore, maintaining the peace is a very high priority.

All of this begs the question, "Is this what Jesus had in mind?" When commissioning the disciples, through the parables, observing his ministry, listening to his teaching....Jesus did not appear to be overly concerned about pleasing the disciples. In fact, the disciples often tried to get Jesus to tone it down, afraid he would run off potential members. Jesus described life in the kingdom as including denial of self, taking up one's cross, giving all for the pearl of great price, and laying down one's life for one's friends. We have to ask how much church-as-we-have-known-it, with varying levels of capitulation to consumer culture, is what Jesus had in mind.

CHAPTER TWELVE
THE RISE OF SACRED PARTNERING

The first two years of presenting these three big moves to groups of clergy and lay persons, this third move was called "Consumer Culture to Covenant Culture." I am familiar with church covenants, having seen them in churches from when I was a child onward. Mostly these were descriptions of how a particular faith community intended to live out their common faith journey. Though church covenants were created with positive intent and hopeful outlooks, most became only words on paper, often glued inside the back cover of hymnals or attached to the church constitution and by-laws. Rarely were they living documents. Though church covenants are not often used well, they do capture the intent of what's needed to form robust faith communities in the 21st century.

Wording....words communicate meaning (as we have already discussed). So the recognition that the word "covenant" may describe what we need, also requires the recognition that this word is too laden with negative associations. Instead we need new wording for this new century.

Finding new wording is ideally done by exploring the need at hand. Here is what we are juxtaposing to the consumer culture which has crept into our understanding of life in faith communities. We desperately, clearly, and emphatically need one another in order to live as disciples of Jesus Christ who are joining God in the transformation of this world. This need awareness drives us to a very focused question. This is the bottom line question when it comes to how we are to be church to one another:

What kind of faith community develops invigorated disciples who join God's movement in the world?

This is the focal question which will help us identify what community in God's church might be. So, how can we relate with each other in this faith community in order to further our development as disciples while growing more missional? What do we need from one another in order to be church in this Postmodern context? As already mentioned, church-as-we-have-known-it does not seem to have within it the elements needed to sustain Christ-followers in our current world. This doesn't mean church has been wrong or bad, it simply means that church-as-we-have-known-it was designed for a different place, time, and cultural context. What's needed from church community now?

When faith communities engage this focal question, they are exploring *Sacred Partnering*. They are considering being in relationship with God and church. These relationships contain an element of mystery. These people are somehow joined together as spiritual kin. The Bible describes the relationship between Christ-followers in familial terms; brothers and sisters. What makes previously unrelated and disconnected people become nearly like family? This is something of a mystery; Holy Spirit work. We are entering the sphere of the sacred when we talk this way. Relationships evolving to this level require something beyond typical human experience - something sacred.

Not only are these relationships sacred, but they are also partnerships. As we have noted, the word "membership" has been co-opted to communicate one's relationship to an organization, which may or may not be sacred. Membership may simply be an organizational term, with organizational rights and privileges. Membership infers a transactional perspective. One receives the rights and privileges conferred with membership when one pays the appropriate dues or fulfills the expected responsibilities. Partnerships are different. Partnerships are formed when people join themselves around a mission. Partners choose to be in relationship with one another without the quid pro quo expectations of contracts. Life partners commit to be with one another through thick and thin, good and bad, for better or worse.

Placing these two words together (Sacred Partnerships) raises the dignity, necessity, and significance of life in this 21st century faith community to new heights. Previously church relationships typically did not involve this level of participation and involvement. But previously the context of our lives was far different. Now, in order to sustain disciple identity and missional movement, we need more from each other. We need sacred partnerships.

Those old Church Covenants plastered on the wall of ancient looking church buildings....they were not always irrelevant documents. At one time they served a function in the life of a church; providing guidance for how the church would be in relationship with each other. Even so, those former Covenants tended to focus on moral behavior. Now the church needs something different from our faith communities. We need partnerships, immersed in God, which actually help us live as disciples who join God on mission in our time and beyond.

I've searched for the perfect metaphor or description for sacred partnerships. My search did not result in a singular description, discovering five instead. Evidently, we need multiple views of the kind of community needed to cultivate and activate sacred partnerships. The following descriptions are of the kinds of faith communities we need to help shape life together as the Beloved Community.

Identity Forming Community
As we have seen already, our calling to become Christ-following disciples who join God on mission in the world is full of challenge. Living like Jesus is not hard to understand, it's just hard to live. As I mentioned before, I can live as a cultural Christian without much effort. But living as a Christ-follower...that's another story. I'm very sure that I can't do this on my own. Even with an extremely supportive faith community, the way is narrow. So, how can we relate with each other in this faith community in order to further our development as disciples and joining God more fully on mission? Perhaps it is time to reclaim an old practice from our faith traditions (Christian community). Perhaps it's time to consider what we need from one another as church in order to be church in the world wherein we find ourselves.

Fortunately, God continually provides for God's people. We call God's provision the Church. It began when small groups of disciples started gathering in the synagogues for prayer soon after the resurrection. Soon thereafter they began gathering in each other's homes, sharing meals. Their sense of community and common mission was so strong that personal ownership of possessions became less important to them. They began to consider themselves as faith community people, before thinking of their individual needs. Powerful things happened among these people. Consider this description from Acts 2:43-47:

> *"Awe came upon everyone, because many wonders and signs were being done by the apostles. All who believed were together and had all things in common; they would sell their possessions and goods and distribute the proceeds to all, as any had need. Day by day, as they spent much time together in the temple, they broke bread at home and ate their food with glad and generous hearts, praising God and having the goodwill of all the people. And day by day the Lord added to their number those who were being saved."(NRSV)*

Surely we romanticize the early church. As the months and years unfolded, conflict became a part of their experience. Whenever people are involved in something, there will be some level of disagreement, as there certainly was in the early church. Even so, this Acts description paints a picture of rich connection and community. What an invigorated group. They believed so much in the gospel that everything else lowered on the importance scale or priority list. The group itself was gathered around a mission which was so profound that identity developed. We can imagine those early Christ followers saying something like, "Now **these** are my people."

This kind of identity marker; this kind of awareness of a closely connected faith community was present in the mother faith of Christ-followers. The prophet Jeremiah describes God's new covenant with the Hebrews this way:

> *The days are surely coming, says the Lord, when I will make a new covenant with the house of Israel and the house of Judah. It will not be like the covenant that I made with their ancestors when I took them by the hand to bring them out of the land of Egypt—a covenant that they broke, though I was their husband, says the Lord. But this is the covenant that I will make with the house of Israel after those days, says the Lord: I will put my law within them, and I will write it on their hearts; and **I will be their God, and they shall be my people.** No longer shall they teach one another, or say to each other, 'Know the Lord,' for they shall all know me, from the least of them to the greatest, says the Lord; for I will forgive their iniquity, and remember their sin no more." Jeremiah 31:31-34 (NRSV)*

This statement, "I will be their God, and they shall be my people," describes sacred partnering relationships which form identity. It's like God is declaring who we all are in relation to each other. We are in community with each other. Our identities are defined through our interconnections. We ARE God's people.

A couple of New Testament writers import this phrase into their context. Paul, in 2 Corinthians 6 quotes this new covenant from Jeremiah. Then the preacher in Hebrews 8 also quotes the same passage. They are describing this new identity for disciples of Jesus Christ in relation to each other and to God. They now are a distinct people, living in relationship with God.

As I'm writing this, the Pew Research Center published its large survey regarding Christian participation in the United States called, "America's Changing Religious Landscape."[1] Those of us who work with Christian churches and denominations, as well as any person paying attention to the religious movement in America, are already anecdotally aware of the decline of participation in Christian churches. This research by the Pew Research Center clearly confirms our observations and experiences. The population which identifies as Christian and participates in Christian churches is shrinking...quickly. Between 2007 and 2014, those who self-identify as Christian dropped from 78.4% to 70.6%. During this same period those who self-identify as "Unaffiliated" rose from 16.1% to 22.8%. Interestingly, out of this grouping, those who identify as "Nothing in Particular" rose from 12.1% to 15.8%.

The rise of the Nones (Spiritual but not religious) occurred a few years ago, and now the appearance of the Dones (church leaders who drop out in frustration), adds nuance to the Pew Research. Clearly there are increasing numbers of people in the United States who are withdrawing from Christian self-identification.

We have a family friend who is looking for a church. She's new to this area, moving here after a divorce, ready to start fresh. After visiting many churches, she is settling into one with a very different theological viewpoint and approach to community compared to the church from where she came. We found ourselves curious about this choice, gently inquiring. Our friend says she really doesn't care much about what they believe. Instead, she is looking for a community of faith to engage. The relationships are what matters to her.

All of this alerts me to two insights. First, the movement out of churches indicates that many are finding the way we do relationships and community in church unsatisfying. Evidently there is not sufficient sacred partnering around the mission. The sense of community is insufficient for sustaining group cohesion. Second, our friend reminds me that we human beings need one another. She's willing to sacrifice in the area of belief systems in order to gain community. We are social creatures, built for interaction and engagement with those of our kind. The human family is designed for interconnection. We need robust faith communities, which engage people and facilitate active interconnection in order to be God's people. Simultaneously, frustration with church community as we have known it is increasing, while longing for deep engaged sacred partnerships is rising.

Frequent or periodic dislocation from place during the 20th century created nomadic lifestyles for many Americans. A logical unintended consequence is the evolution of relationship nomads. Other factors conspire with geographical dislocation to loosen relational connections. Technology, with all its wonderful uses and benefits, introduces distance into what were formerly face-to-face relationships. Most of the time people email me first before calling by phone, if we even ever talk by phone. Technology allows us to move quickly, at the expense of relational connection. Affluence also allows us to feel like we need one another less. When it comes to survival needs, and even personal preferences, the more affluent we become, the less we depend on others. Well, at least the less we depend on others in voluntary type relationships. We are actually more dependent on others whom we pay to do for us or supply our needs. Geographical dislocation, technological advances, and affluence are only some of the factors weakening the sense of community in our Postmodern world.

Being social creatures, we long for relational connection. The old proverb, "A sorrow shared is halved, and a joy shared is doubled," describes well our desire for others with whom to share life's journey. We want travelling partners; people with whom to ride the river.

This need for relational community is not new or unique to our time. The apostle Peter, writing to the exiles of the dispersion, falls all over himself informing and reassuring these exiles that they are part of a living spiritually based community.

> "But you are a chosen race, a royal priesthood, a holy nation, God's own people, in order that you may proclaim the mighty acts of him who called you out of darkness into his marvelous light. Once you were not a people, but now you are God's people; once you had not received mercy, but now you have received mercy." I Peter 2:9-10 (NRSV)

Look at all the identity-forming names Peter gives them – A chosen race, a royal priesthood, a holy nation, God's own people. He pulls from Jewish history and theology to encourage identity in this new community of faith. "Once you were not a people." Once you were not part of this faith community; once you did not have this new identity as one of God's people called the church. "But now you ARE God's people." Peter encourages this new identity as one of God's people called the church. We can imagine those early Christ-followers who experienced the great dispersion soon after the resurrection...having to move away from their communities of origin, becoming geographical nomads due to persecution and prejudice, hearing those sweet words..."Once you were not a people, but now you are God's people." Now they are part of the Beloved Community. Thanks be to God.

This is what we need from Postmodern churches. We need a people, a community, an identity as part of this organism called church in order to sustain robust spirituality and Christ-following.

Geographical Anchoring Community
This second faith community description may seem contradictory given all our talk about joining God on mission; God inspiring a movement in the world. Actually, connecting with a particular context and geographical community is a natural extension of the Missional Church Movement. This is part of the intent of the Missional Church Movement, to join God in a particular place, announcing the reign of God and recognizing the presence of God's kingdom in a context.

A strange thing is happening in the city where we live. Well, actually, we live in the suburbs. We live in one of those small towns which used to be "way out there," away from the city. Now it's a bedroom community, with people living here but driving there for work. The strange thing happening is the reverse of suburban flight. People are moving into the city. A downtown renaissance of sorts is starting. Where once people were eager to flee to the suburbs, now young professionals, students, singles, and families are reversing the flow. For many reasons, the place to be is changing, with the city pulling people to it rather than repelling them. Our city is not unique. This trend toward urban dwelling is growing and gaining speed as we speak. Part of the motivation for this flow toward the city is a desire for greater engagement with others in community; for a geographically anchored place to call one's own.

When we step back and look at demographic trends over time, we recognize we are living in a very transient society. During the latter half of the twentieth century, the trend for those wanting to succeed was to get one's education and then launch off into one's career. This included a willingness to go where the job, organization, or corporation sent. I remember one man's introduction of himself as a visioning team was forming. "I was a corporate nomad most of my career. Every 3 years we picked up and moved to where the company sent us." Corporate nomads...Many in North America have lived nomadic lives due to the transience of their vocations. This, and other factors, made it possible for suburbs with sprawling subdivisions to rise. One could sell a house in one subdivision in one state and buy another house in a very similar subdivision in another state.

For many years in this country churches were linked to places. They were neighborhood or community churches, with deep roots in their local community. Their existence was symbiotic with the community's existence. "Parishes" describes a geographical area with people who shared a similar location in common. They were rooted to place.

The rise of the suburban lifestyle introduced new elements into church life. Given this lifestyle for many in the twentieth century, the church was quick to adapt to this understanding of life. Disciples were more transient, coming and going depending on their job assignments and opportunities. Disciples were also more mobile. They were conditioned to travel distances to work (suburbs to the city), so they transferred this experience to their church life. Churches then became more regional. They were "outsourced" from neighborhoods to more of a franchise model (like all the other consumer oriented organizations around them). Some even developed satellites of their franchises in other suburban communities.

Now in the 21st century we are seeing the reverse of these trends. People are moving from the suburb to the city. "Go local" is now common language. We are recognizing ourselves as tourists in our own communities, hardly attached to place at all. This has created a strong hunger in humankind for place; for a place to call home. Postmodern Christ-followers hunger for a faith community which is deeply rooted in its place on the planet, forming a strong bond with its local community.

The opportunity this presents to the 21st century church is to "go local." Postmodern pilgrims are weary of being disconnected from place due to frequent moves with its accompanying displacement. Though not everyone has complete control over how long they live in one community, many of us want to engage with our "place" where we are while we can. We want to live as if this is our place, our community, for the foreseeable future. Some are making the choice to sacrifice career advancement, staying in a job so that they can become more rooted in their community. The Postmodern church can serve as an anchoring community. We already see our church communities as spiritually and relationally anchoring for us. We become the church gathered for worship and Christian formation. This anchors our faith and fuels our spiritual tanks for being the church dispersed. Postmodern churches can become anchors in another very tangible way. Those faith communities with buildings are identified with a particular place in their community. It is time to see the church (people and building) as a part of that community, as a part of the local culture. In order to live as invigorated disciples in our current context, we need church to grow connected to place. We need our churches to embrace the local, investing in its community context, being a part of and contributing to the shaping of our local contexts. This will help anchor Postmodern Christ-followers in the 21st century.

Personal Transformation Community
>   *"It seems only fair, for example, to ask that the members of the body of Christ look and act differently from those who are not part of the beloved community. They should seem like 'resident aliens,' according to authors Stanley Hauerwas and William H. Willimon, a part of a 'colony' more than a congregation. The Christian community should not feel at home in the world, as if it is a 'voluntary organization of like-minded individuals.'"[2]*
>   *Robin R. Meyers*

Is a Personal Transformation Community the same as the first big shift; becoming disciples? Yes and no. Developing disciples or Christian Formation certainly includes personal transformation, yet is larger than only personal transformation. In fact, a weakness in some Christian traditions is the tendency to see disciple development as limited to the personal piety or holiness of individuals. This perspective encourages the pursuit of more holy lifestyles (a very good pursuit) while inadvertently truncating the gospel to the private personal piety realm. Disciple development includes working for social justice; for no less than the transformation of the world. Partnering with God to announce the kingdom and contributing to its appearance on earth as it is in heaven is a major activity of discipleship.

By focusing on personal transformation here, we are identifying a part of discipleship. This is the area of life which does include personal piety and transformation. This is the part of our faith wherein we have aha moments, where we wake up to our new identity in Christ. The Apostle Paul described it well, saying,

> *"From now on, therefore, we regard no one from a human point of view; even though we once knew Christ from a human point of view, we know him no longer in that way. So if anyone is in Christ, there is a new creation: everything old has passed away; see, everything has become new!"* [2]
>
> *Corinthians 5:16-18 (NRSV)*

What kind of faith community cultivates or incubates disciples who are personally growing and being transformed by the Spirit of God? What role do sacred partnerships play in helping this new creation blossom and bloom? How shall we relate to one another when we want to encourage this kind of personal transformation in each other?

This is not quick work. Personal transformation toward the reflection of Jesus Christ is the long slow work of salvation. This is sanctification work, to use a theological word. We need communities of faith who can engage disciples in this work with patient intentionality, knowing this journey takes a lifetime to complete.

Ronald Heifitz, Marty Linskey, and Alexander Grashow gave the world a great gift through their book, *The Practice Of Adaptive Leadership*.[3] Adapting is the primary activity needed by organizations who will survive and thrive in our Postmodern context. One of their metaphors serves us well when considering what we need from church in order to engage transformation:

My mother was fond of canning vegetables each summer. I remember seeing the pressure cooker on the stove, watching the small release valve bounce up and down as the steam whistled out. I'm not an expert on the preserving process, but we can identify insights to guide us as we lead faith communities from this rich metaphor.

- What comes out (when the process is done well) is very different than what went in (transformation)
- The temperature must remain hot enough, for long enough, in order to break down the ingredients and transform these ingredients into something else
- The temperature can become too hot or cool, ruining the ingredients
- Pressure is necessary to transform the ingredients
- The right amount of pressure is required; with too little or too much ruining the ingredients

This pressure cooker metaphor reminds us that the

transformation process is tricky business, requiring good process and necessary structure.

What then does this tell us about what's needed from a faith communities who practice sacred partnering? Church becomes a personal transformation community when it provides the holding environment (pressure cooker) necessary for us to become transformed into disciples of Jesus Christ. To do this, church must hold several paradoxical dynamics in tension within the holding environment (faith community).

Sometimes continuums are very useful for describing paradoxical truths. We need from our faith communities dynamics which seem diametrically opposed, even though each is connected and necessary. These dynamics are lived out in tension with each other, contributing to personal transformation of disciples.

Acceptance _____ Challenge

What's our theology say? Does God require us to change before accepting us? No, God accepts us, loves us, just as we are. Phillip Yancey's book, *What's So Amazing About Grace?* [4], promotes the idea that we cannot do anything to make God love us more. We cannot be good enough, or outstanding enough, or anything else enough to increase God's love. Nor can we do anything to decrease God's love for us. We can't be corrupt enough, or cynical enough, or anything else enough to decrease God's love. God simply loves us. This love is based on the identity and character of God, not on our worthiness. God's love is gift, pure and simple. Our actions have nothing to do with God's love. So the opportunity before us is to receive God's love, day by day, deeper into our beings. This is acceptance.

Simultaneously, God loves us too much to leave us as we are. God sees potential in us. God believes in us. God has hopes and dreams for us; for who we can become. In fact, God has a mission for each of us; a calling so to speak. God calls us to get up and go out the door, joining God on mission in the world. In so doing, God intends for us to lay aside the sin and weights which hold us down. God wants to transform us into reflections of our Lord, encouraging the image of Christ residing within us to shine through. This is our challenge – to become more Christ-like human beings. This is challenge.

When I served as a marriage and family therapist, this tension between acceptance and challenge played out right in front of me all the time. Couples would come into the therapy office, typically wanting me to help him or her change the other (challenge the other to step up). The problem, as each saw it, was that his or her spouse needed changing. Ironically, the pathway to change typically began with acceptance rather than challenge. The more he or she accepted the other as is, the more the other wanted to change in order to please the spouse. Acceptance and challenge resided on the same continuum, requiring doses of both in order to facilitate growth and change. Faith communities who practice sacred partnering purposefully practice acceptance and challenge in their community life.

Grace _____ Expectation

Yes, these are similar to the previous continuum, but different. Acceptance is about who we are while grace is about what we do. Challenge calls us to become different, while expectation is about our actions in relation to God and one another.

In order to change or be transformed as disciples, we need grace.

The Christian Church has practiced confession for centuries. We believe that confession is good for the soul. Many churches include an opportunity for confession as part of their worship gatherings. As a pastor, I'm amazed how the space we are occupying turns sacred when I hear the private confession of a disciple. Sometimes he begins with, "I've never shared this with anyone, but I just have to get it out in the open." Other times she starts with, "This thing I've been carrying so long is eating away my soul – it's time to bring it before God." Sometimes we need another person to hear our confession and help us take it to God. Then grace happens.

Who are the people in your life who will help you back to your feet after you stumble and fall? Who are those who will react with sorrow and empathy when you fail rather than anger or criticism? Who is it who sees your mistakes as learning and growth experiences, rather than terminal actions which must end your relationship with them? We all need people like this in our lives, people who practice God's grace as sacred partners.

At the very same time, we need people who expect really good things from us. We need people around us who expect us to live like disciples of Jesus Christ, who anticipate we will love God and people. Invigorated faith communities actually expect disciples to grow, change, develop and become little-Christs for the world. They discuss what it means to be a faith community together. They describe the kinds of relationships toward which they aspire. "When we become more Christ-like in this church, how will that change how we currently relate with each other?" If the answer is, "nothing will change," then your faith community is not engaging the teachings of Jesus with any depth. God loves us too much to leave us as we are – and one way God has provided for us to change is to rub shoulders with other disciples in this group of people we call church. When one stumbles and fails, they practice grace, lifting one back to the pilgrim pathway. When one grows complacent or arrogant, they describe their expectations of Christ-like relating, calling each other to more Spirit-based living.

Comfort _____ Celebration

Given the transience in our culture, many of us live far from our extended families. In fact we may be very new to our community when crisis occurs. One of the great gifts of sacred partnering is a community with whom to experience life. There are times when we crash. There are those times when crisis looms, grief descends, or injury happens. That's when sacred partners care for each other, being the presence of Christ to each other. This provides great comfort to disciples.

On the other end of this continuum are those times when life exceeds our expectations. With whom in life can you share your joys and wins? Who are the people who can step outside themselves enough to allow your successes to be about you, rather than turning the focus to themselves? Sacred partners rejoice when one of their own does well or experiences something really good. They are able to give the gift of celebration. Sacred partnering communities can hold comfort and celebration together as they live out their faith journeys.

World Transformation Community
> *Thy kingdom come, thy will be done on earth as it is in heaven.*
>
> Jesus Christ, Matthew's Gospel[5]

What did he mean? What's this Lord's Prayer, recited by millions each Sunday and many every day, telling us? Jesus, as described in Matthew's gospel, teaches his disciples to pray in this way. Jesus teaches us to pray that God's kingdom will come on earth. Now, did Jesus really believe this could happen? Did he anticipate that at some point in time, God's intentions, dreams, hopes for this world would be actualized in real life? I guess one's eschatology needs to be consulted before answering this question. My view is that God would not ask us to pray for something which has zero chance of happening. This would seem to be an exercise in frustrated futility. My view is that God intends for God's kingdom to come on earth as it is in heaven. The process of God's kingdom coming on earth involves us, God's Church, partnering with God in this mission.

If this is so, then when we pray this prayer, we are joining ourselves with God in God's mission to bring the kingdom of God to earth as it is in heaven. What a radical prayer. And, a somewhat radical faith community is required to cultivate this kind of Christ-follower. This kind of faith community is on mission with God focused on cultivating no less than world transformation. This faith community believes the world is not as it should be in its current expression, but it is not yet what it shall be in its transformed kingdom expression. This faith community is on mission with God in this world, engaging in world transformation.

We have already explored how personal transformation is part of the Christian movement's purpose. As we are being transformed personally, we are called to participate in God's transformation of the world. This includes the structures, policies, practices of our society. This is participation in the public square, addressing the large scale injustices in our society. Recently our family was discussing the effect human activity has on climate change. Our children were asking why some politicians and others in this country deny climate change is happening, in spite of overwhelming evidence to the contrary. We discussed how everything is interconnected – politics, funding, corporations, etc. Heavy investment in the status quo, even when it is contrary to the Biblical mandate to be effective stewards of the earth, is difficult to change. Our children see the Church as having a moral mandate to address this injustice, working to fulfill God's calling to be faithful stewards of God's creation. This, and many other Postmodern Era issues, calls the Church to join God's mission to bring the kingdom to earth as it is in heaven. We are called to work for our personal transformation, while also joining God in world transformation.

This brings us back to our focus question:
What kind of faith community develops invigorated disciples who join God's movement in the world? World transformation faith communities call us up out of ourselves. We need our churches to call us out of our culturally encouraged self-centeredness into a less self-focused way of living.

We were in the process of identifying God's calling for their next steps as a congregation. They were wrestling with their desire to join God on mission, but with very little idea of what that would look like. Most of their conversation focused on alleviating specific human needs; food, shelter, resources. Eventually the pastor of the church spoke up. "We are really good at providing things for those with tangible material needs. But here we are, surrounded by this affluent community. And most of us in this room have our basic needs met, with plenty left over for leisure activities. We know how to care for the poor, but we don't have a clue what to do in partnership with the affluent who surround our church campus." This pastor's statement led to a fascinating conversation. We are used to providing answers or material things for those in very obvious need. What do we do with people who don't appear to have such obvious needs?

I've been wrestling with this question myself for quite a long time now. I've come to an answer which is giving me guidance, even if it remains incomplete. I believe that what we middle-class and affluent industrialized first-world folk need is to join God on mission. In other words, we need to rise up out of our self-focused lives and give back to the world. Sure, it's very enjoyable to have what we have and be able to do what we do. Simultaneously, life is not all about us. I find myself thinking of that passage in Luke's gospel wherein Jesus is describing the responsibility of servants who are faithful and diligent in their work, serving in their master's household. "From everyone to whom much has been given, much will be required; and from the one to whom much has been entrusted, even more will be demanded." We need faith communities who will call us to rise up out of our self-focused lives to participate with God in world transformation.

Yet, I find myself very weary of watered down church expectations. Most congregations seem to seek the lowest threshold possible, the least common denominator, and the lesser motives of humanity when it comes to inviting participation in their faith community. It seems that churches are so afraid of offending, losing, or otherwise diminishing their institutional strength, that they will lower the bar even below ground if it will get people in the door. I find myself asking again, "Is this what Jesus gave his life for? Is this what Jesus had in mind? Shouldn't we organize ourselves for calling out to the higher motives and better impulses of humanity?" I find myself so weary of churches "dumbing-down" the expectations for disciples. The result when we do is a very tepid, boring, and impotent faith.

But, as noted before, involving ourselves with others is so messy. Becoming engaged with others is unpredictable, scary, and pushes our boundaries. Shane Claiborne, that Postmodern prophet of The Simple Way in Philadelphia, makes me laugh each time I hear him speak. Claiborne grew up in East Tennessee, raised by committed Christian parents who were very engaged with their traditional denominationally based church. When their son went off to college in Philadelphia, he discovered a completely different way of living in the Way of Jesus. He became involved with the poor and marginalized, realizing he had a responsibility for making the world a better place. His faith journey progressed from only privatized, personal piety to public, social justice work. In one of his presentations he made a comment something like, "I met Jesus and he ruined my life." Claiborne is describing how taking the gospel seriously disturbed his cultural Christianity, calling him out of himself to another way of living. No longer could he stay the same, which made him uncomfortable. Ultimately, he is discovering a very spiritually satisfying way to live, yet it included sacrifice of comforts to which he was accustomed.

What if churches began to actually practice real expectations for their disciples? What if we expected one another to actively join God on mission in the world? How would we even start?

First, Christ-followers involved in traditionally-based congregations may need debriefing. We may have to let go of our understanding of church before moving on. Darrell Guder helps us deconstruct church as we have known it. *"We must surrender the self-conception of the church as a voluntary association of individuals and live by the recognition that we are a communal body of Christ's followers, mutually committed and responsible to one another and to the mission Jesus set us upon at his resurrection."*[6] This is the practice of sacred partnering.

Then after letting go, we must embrace new expectations of ourselves and one another as Christ-followers who join God on mission. Guder describes this next step, *"The calling of the church to be missional – to be a sent community – leads the church to step beyond the given cultural forms that carry dubious assumptions about what the church is, what its public role should be, and what its voice should sound like."*[7]

My colleague Doug Cushing is the founding pastor of a new church in Wilmington, NC called The Bridge Presbyterian Church. As they were beginning, he described their desire to incarnationally engage their community. This new church wants to avoid having a "missions program" or missions committee who organizes the church around mission work. This is new ground for most of us, so they are giving themselves permission to experiment. As they started, they did not begin a traditional Sunday School for Christian formation. Instead, they started sermon-based small groups which meet during the week. This is one very intentional way they cultivate one another as disciples. In the process of initiating Christian-formation small groups, they stumbled onto the idea of inserting the missional impulse into each small group. Now each small group is encouraged and expected to engage its community, discovering ways to partner with God on mission. They are given a small amount of money from the church budget which can be used if they find it helpful.

Regardless, each small group purposefully pursues disciple development and missional engagement. Expectations for being on mission are structured into this new church's DNA. Sacred partnering includes being World Transformation Communities.

Partnership Pilgrimage Community
Did we save the best description of a new kind of faith community for last? Well, it seems like it's extremely important. By now you know that I am clear on my inability to sustain living in the Way of Jesus on my own. There is no doubt in my mind, nor in my experience, that I must have travelling partners to sustain this pilgrimage. Yes, there are times when we take a stand alone. Yet those times are very rare. We human beings are social creatures who function best when part of a significant community with supportive ties.

Jesus seemed to encourage strong relational connections in the body of Christ. During the Farewell Discourse, Jesus gives the new commandment we discussed earlier.

> *"Little children, I am with you only a little longer. You will look for me; and as I said to the Jews so now I say to you, 'Where I am going, you cannot come.' I give you a new commandment, that you love one another. Just as I have loved you, you also should love one another. By this everyone will know that you are my disciples, if you have love for one another."*
>
> *John 13:33-35 (NRSV)*

Clearly, the way to determine whether we are disciples, according to this passage, is how we love one another in the Body of Christ (church). When lived, this new commandment leads to close

179

relational connections among Christ's disciples; sacred partnerships.

Now, compare this new commandment to your church experience. There are some churches who have found ways to practice significant relational connections. Traditional denominationally based churches often experience much looser connections. I can imagine disciples reading this and saying to themselves, "Love one another....I hardly know these people." Worshipping together once a week, serving on a committee together, or participating in social events on the church campus...these are good, but not adequate for creating relationships which support our Christian pilgrimage in this challenging Postmodern context.

Again, we need a warning here. When we go deeper with people, when we invest in people, when we engage in authentic relationships, we can't control what happens. Life can grow messy. Just like when we join God on mission in the world, life also grows complicated when we engage partner disciples more significantly. Robin Meyers in his boundary-pushing book, captures the yen and yang of comfort/discomfort when disciples authentically engage each other. *"Likewise, we should tell anyone who joins a church that they have just entered into a strange and bewildering covenant of blessed inconvenience."*[8]

For those looking for a sequestered life, removed from engagement and interaction with others...well, this partnership pilgrimage community won't be for you. Certainly there are times when we need and find sanctuary in our church experience (perhaps literally in the sanctuary). There are times when we pull aside on retreat, either solo or with our faith community, for respite and connecting with God in deeper ways. Yet, these are temporary time. Most of our faith community experience is just that – community experience.

We were watching a video series as part of a discussion group in the church wherein I participated. The video was of a gathering of theologians discussing their views on church. The camera shifted to one theologian who worked as a pastoral counselor...someone very familiar with the brokenness of humanity. Her comment was striking at the time. "Church is where we learn to tolerate one another," she said with a sly smile. Church is the crucible community within which we learn to love others. So be aware that shifting church towards becoming a partnership pilgrimage community brings risks. None of us will emerge unchanged, or perhaps even unscathed. But when we form community of faith relationships at this level, we find our souls enriched and our strength amplified.

Most of the time I do my running by myself. I enjoy the time away and alone, enjoying reflection time while I run. Afterwards, I'm ready to re-engage others and the world again. Sometimes though, I run with others. Recently my young adult son was home, so we went to the woods for a trail run. My goal was to complete the distance without having to walk. His goal was to practice patience, slowing down enough to stay with me. Previously, I tried running the same trail, having to walk several times. This time, running with my son, I ran the entire trail. Toward the run's end, when I wanted to walk, his encouragement and simply his presence kept me moving. I was reminded of how sharing a run with another decreases the challenges and increases the enjoyment. I'm a far better runner when running with another rather than alone. Partnership makes the impossible more possible.

Sacred Partnerships

Sometimes I think the Monastics had it right. Living communally, sharing resources, engaging life together with pilgrimage partners over time. There is something very attractive in this for Postmodern pilgrims from highly individualistic focused cultures. Even so, most of us are not able, willing, nor planning to join monastic communities. Our lives are centered in our communities, appearing more typical than not.

This reality though does not diminish our need for sacred partnerships. Our need is just as much, or perhaps greater, when it comes to partnerships around living in the Way of Jesus in our context.

CHAPTER THIRTEEN
MAKING THE SHIFT TOWARD SACRED PARTNERING

Poor Pygmalion.

He was the Greek character from Ovid's ancient narrative poem called Metamorphoses. Pygmalion was a victim of his own talent; such a gifted sculptor that he fell in love with the statue he sculpted.

Modern researchers love this ancient story of Pygmalion; finding in it a great metaphor explaining what they've discovered in social science research. This is where the phrase, "Self-fulfilling Prophecy," originates. Evidently, when we believe something will happen, or more accurately, when we believe someone is a certain way, then we unconsciously arrange our behavior in accordance with this belief. When we believe a person is witty, then we tend to laugh at his remarks. When we believe she is smart, we think her insights are brilliant. When we believe they are full of potential, then we present them with opportunities to demonstrate their ability. This is the Pygmalion Effect.[1]

The reverse of the Pygmalion is also true. We might call this Pygmalion's evil twin. The Golem Effect happens when we believe less about a person or group, thinking he/she/they are destined to failure, are not very bright, or are stuck in unhelpful patterns. When we persist in the Golem Effect, seeing our faith communities as unwilling to change (or other negative perspectives), then we unconsciously relate to our faith community as if this is the gospel truth. This is the Golem Effect.

What if Pygmalion and Golem went to church?
More accurately, these two are already there.
The Golem Effect appeared recently in a consultation with a pastor. He's concerned about the church, coming for a consultation on what might be done to help. I could summarize his perspective about them this way, "They are happy as they are. They don't want any help from anyone outside the congregation, though they are declining quickly. I have very little hope they will change." I don't doubt this pastor's description of this church, based on what he described. But what will happen if this pastor retains this point of view? Unconsciously, he will select evidence from his experience with this congregation which confirms this viewpoint. Yes, this is the classic self-fulfilling prophecy. Certainly this pastor cannot change this congregation simply by believing differently about them. Yet just as certainly, this pastor is unlikely to participate in an effective change process while believing these things about them, thereby squandering his leadership opportunity. This is the Golem Effect at church.

The Pygmalion Effect is at church too.
We are working with a congregation which has declined. They are a lovely bunch of people, with great love for each other and their community. Yet, they are older and discouraged and unsure about the future. In our discussions, one person piped up and said, "We received a phone call from the new church starting in our

community. They wondered if we would sell them our facility."
This comment triggered a new insight for this church. They began
to play with this new way of looking at themselves. What is it
about this place, and then about us as a people, that a new
church would see this and us as assets? This led to recognition of
many great assets among them: a building and property without a
mortgage, a sizeable group of people who meet regularly for
worship and love one another, a willingness to change given their
reality, etc. When they looked at themselves as a new church
developer would (You mean I don't have to go find a core group
to start this church? They are already there, along with this great
facility? Luxury!), their appreciation for potential fruitful ministry
rose dramatically. This is a church who is now corporately
practicing the Pygmalion Effect.

I believe it's time to use what humanity knows to strengthen our
faith communities. Actually, we are already part of a faith
movement which provides everything we need to practice the
Pygmalion Effect. Throughout the Old and New Testaments, our
spiritual kinfolks frequently seized the opportunity to call people
to a better way of life, all the while believing God would provide
what they needed to follow God's call toward the promised land
(notwithstanding Jonah).

Perhaps it's time for faith communities to become high
expectation organizations. Maybe it's time we start believing in
the best in one another. Perhaps it's time to establish sacred
partnerships which help us do faith community in ways which
advance our faith. We are not interested raising expectations for
community simply to become high expectation organizations.
What we are really interested in is answering this driving, focus
question: *What kind of faith community develops invigorated*

disciples who join God's movement in the world? We are too far into this Postmodern transition to live out of duty or compulsion (as if that ever worked anyway). Instead we are eager to discover how to become invigorated faith communities who include robust interactional relationships as a part of their identity. Again, what kind of faith community develops invigorated disciples who join God's movement in the world? You are invited to make the shift toward sacred partnering by engaging the following practices.

Cultivating a Taste for Sacred Partnering
Again, there is a reason this third shift is the third shift. Disciples have to believe there is a need for more robust relationships among them before they want these kinds of relationships. If we try changing the language or otherwise moving toward sacred partnerships prematurely, disciples perceive this as only semantics. You might be changing the labels and descriptions, but disciples will expect to continue doing church as they have always done.

Before making this third shift, the first two big moves must be engaged. We begin by shifting from member identity to disciple identity. We continue by moving from attractional churches to missional churches. Then disciples are sensitized to the necessity for robust, significant spiritually-laced relationships. These first two shifts are huge. When disciples try them, with their typical levels of support in place, they will experience some level of failure. Then they are ready for sacred partnering. Then their appetite for sacred partnering is activated.

Not only are we driven to sacred partnering by our need. When we taste of the Lord, we find that the Lord is good. When we accept our identity as disciples and begin engaging our world missionally, then our spirits come alive. Once we experience it, there is no going back. We can't stuff this genie back in the bottle. Michael Frost describes this well. *"We have been swept up into a new awareness of the mission Dei, the unstoppable program of God's unfurling kingdom on earth, and we can't even conceive of how to control it, package it, or franchise it. One cannot be infected by this wonderful life-giving virus and remain content with church-business-as-usual."[2]*

Changing Our Language
Are we allowed to "retire" words? Who in our society officially calls it quits for words which no longer hold relevance or usefulness? In fact, how do dictionary publishers decide to include or exclude words from their newer editions? I would imagine frequency and necessity of use are driving factors. Those words which are used in our language survive and thrive, while unused words go the way of all things.

So, let's start a word movement. I invite you to join me in changing your vocabulary, eliminating that-which-shall-no-longer-be-spoken (church membership). Instead, when describing our relationships with one another and to God's Church, let's use the phrase "sacred partnering." As discussed before, the way we describe ourselves and our actions actually forms them. Changing our language is a strong step toward making the shift away from consumer church culture.

We can go ahead and make this shift in our everyday dialogue. But what if we want to go deep; to more officially and organizationally change our language? What would it take to change our New Member Class to a Sacred Partnership Learning Experience? What would we need to do to update our language in our polity; our church documents? What about our website? How would we describe Sacred Partnering there? A sermon series on sacred partnering could raise our awareness.

Contrasting Consumer Culture Versus Sacred Partnering
Sometimes we need to gain an accurate understanding of where we are as congregations. From this assessment we often discover the invigorating challenge which moves us forward into actionable engagement. One effective way to gain perspective into the level of consumer church culture we practice is to listen to the questions which pastors, church staff, and lay leaders discuss. See the following contrasting chart for questions which indicate a tilt one way or the other.

Consumer Church Culture	*Versus*	Sacred Partnership Communities
How happy are our members?		What is God's calling for us as a church?
Are we doing what we can to keep our members happy?		What is God's calling for us as individuals?
How happy are our members with what this church is doing?		How well are we contributing to the development of God's disciples?
Is anyone upset, unsettled, or disgruntled?		What is needed to advance God's mission more fully; comfort or challenge?
Are there any problems we need to fix in order to restore peace?		What needs in this church are being met and what needs require attention?
How can we get people to volunteer more?		What may be holding us back from developing disciples and joining God on mission?

How does this conversation go in your congregation's lay leadership team meetings? How about your pastoral and program staff meetings? What's the focus of your faith community? We suggest you use this exercise to facilitate dialogue among your leadership. By gaining perspective, you can then strategize your next steps toward sacred partnering.

Recognizing that sacred partnering opportunities are a natural part of what you do as church, with intentional engagement as the key

Some things develop because we intentionally focus on them, while others come to life as a result of focusing elsewhere. Sacred partnering is both. When we consider what we currently do as churches, we realize there are many activities which could include sacred partnering. The primary purpose of these activities is not to grow spiritual relationships and connection, yet this happens as a result of these activities. If your congregation is engaging disciple developing and missional action then spiritual connection will happen as a by-product.

The key here is intentional engagement and participation. As is true with any group activity, those who engage and are involved in the group's activities and mission are those who find good connection and satisfying relationships. In one way, we could say that relational connection results from everything we do as a faith community (worship, serving, etc.). Anytime we engage in anything with each other, there is the distinct possibility that relationships will grow. So from the beginning, encourage and expect one another to engage with each other, furthering sacred partnering.

Intentionally create opportunities for spiritually-based relational intimacy to grow, including sharing one's story

As previously noted, sacred partnering opportunities are there in everything we do as faith communities. It's also true that many congregations do not intentionally encourage sacred partnering, which can lead to very loose relational connections.

In addition to what's noted above, what else helps relational intimacy grow? There are many activities we could list: shared worship experiences, serving together to make someone's life better, dialoguing about theological conundrums, making decisions about the faith community. All of these are good and helpful. Yet, to really know and connect with someone, we need to know something of that disciple's story. What's been your journey? How did you come to faith in Christ? What made you want to be a disciple? What have been and are your joys and sorrows? What lights you up, fires your imagination? What drives you these days? Where do you struggle now?

To really know others, there comes a time when we need to hear the other tell his/her story. This doesn't negate the other ways for growing close; rather it enhances them. I've had way too many people tell me they discover relational intimacy far more in Alcoholics Anonymous than they ever do in church. We usually walk away from those conversations with this unfulfilled longing, wishing our church could move to that kind of relational intimacy. Based on the major shifts in our world creating huge challenges for God's Church, we need each other far more than ever before. So, we need intentional opportunities to take our spiritual connections to deeper levels.

Disciple developing small groups are an excellent way to provide this opportunity. We cannot make sacred partnering happen, yet we can place ourselves in situations where it is far more likely. Faith sharing opportunities...wherein people tell their story to others in the faith community, open relational doors. I remember an experiment from Social Psychology class which described how self-disclosure (sharing something personal) by one person naturally elicits self-disclosure by others. We have experienced this in real life. When a friend describes something personal, the impulse to respond with our story about a similar life experience rises up in us. Disciple developing missional churches identify and provide intentional ways for disciples to share their stories with each other.

Teach, train, promote, and encourage this shift from focusing on our individual needs, wants, and preferences to focusing on the collective life of our faith community.
How do we do this? How do we accomplish culture-shift? How do we help a group of people shift from the way they have been conditioned to think by their native culture (high priority on individualism) toward a community of faith perspective? This is spiritual journey kind of work – changing our perspectives on what's important in life.

Preaching, training, teaching...these activities are integral to being church. They are great tools to use for helping culture change. Reframing our perspectives, cultivating new paradigms, learning together...these can become the focus of our Christian formation efforts.

Consider crafting a covenant used to support, advance, and further sacred partnering
I'm not an expert on church covenants. Most I've encountered are

historical artifacts, reviewed for history's sake once in a great while. At the same time, perhaps it's time for us to consider what our pledges to one another are. Remember our focus question, "What kind of faith community develops invigorated disciples who join God's movement in the world?" We could translate this question to, "What do we need from one another in order to become those kinds of disciples?"

Many Christian denominations include liturgy in their membership vows which speaks to this. For most, time has eroded the impact of these vows, rendering them benign. I wonder what you would create if you commissioned a team to craft a statement about what you need from one another in order to live out your collective calling as a faith community?

Engage 90-day and annual check-ins with every disciple
Wise leaders in hospitals, educational institutions, corporations, and small businesses schedule 90-day reviews with new employees. They recognize that the early period of one's employment is a vulnerable time. They are also aware that it costs so much more to go through another interviewing and hiring process than to conserve the current employees. So, they try staying in close contact with employees as they start up with this new organization. In addition, savvy organizations do substantial yearly reviews with all employees.

In church life, the early involvement period is pivotal as well. Those who develop relationships with at least one group in the church are far more likely to grow and develop as disciples. Those who do not connect may not be around for long. Intentionally checking-in with newer disciples provides opportunity to consider relational connection. When faith communities build this into their practice, then everyone knows this is just what we do. But let's not reserve check-ins for only newcomers. Checking-in with every disciple every year provides a great way to further sacred partnering.

CHAPTER FOURTEEN
PERHAPS IT'S TIME

"The more I believe in Jesus and try to live according to his teachings, the less fit I am for being part of the church as I know it (as it's been designed and practiced during the twentieth century)."

Statement made by a sincere Christ-follower
during a discussion about being
part of a robust faith community

It was one of those moments wherein one of THOSE statements is made...a statement which captures the essence of the group's dialogue and sentiment up to this point, usually followed by a weighty silence. This was an informal gathering of people who are trying to find their way regarding church. One middle-aged woman who made the statement above nailed it for the group. She articulated what they were each saying in various ways. Most grew up in church, with great appreciation of the formative role church has played in their lives. These are not newcomers to the faith, but are faithful disciples who regularly participate with their faith communities. Now, more of them are finding it challenging to reconcile the focus of their church with the sayings, parables, and apparent priorities of Jesus in the Bible. They love Jesus – and they are struggling with their church's expression of the Way of Jesus.

Soon after the dialogue above, I was doing visioning work with a large Presbyterian church. During the listening phase of our process, one woman made this remark, "It takes a lot of energy to be a Presbyterian." Her remark was not in answer to a question about being Presbyterian. She made this remark in the context of visioning work; imagining the church of the future. With great weariness she described the last three years. She was on the lay leadership team (Session), which meant she also was assigned to serve as a committee chair. The result was meetings of some kind more than one evening each week. After these three years she expressed great fatigue and a fair dose of frustration regarding being caught up in institutional maintenance. She viewed much of her service to God through these meetings as useless and insignificant. She appeared to be the poster-child for "Post-Traumatic Church Fatigue." I wondered how long she would stay involved with her particular church. (Directions for reading the story above: When you come to the word "Presbyterian," insert your denominational or non-denominational label there. Institutionalism is no respecter of denominations, being more of 20th century church model "ism" rather than being unique to any particular denomination.)

These two experiences with sincere Christ-followers demonstrated again that we are leaving something and taking hold of something else. Disciples are abandoning the twentieth century formatted church, finding it tedious, unwieldy, and insufficient. Simultaneously, disciples are ever more intrigued with the Way of Jesus as the way forward for our broken and hurting world.

So, perhaps it's time.
Perhaps it's time to give ourselves permission.
Perhaps it's time to give ourselves permission to quit church-as-we-have-known-it.
Perhaps it's time to give ourselves permission to quit church-as-we-have-known-it so that we can engage church-as-it-is-becoming.
Perhaps it's time to become a Church powered by renewable energy sources; Holy Spirit Wind.

Can we grant ourselves this kind of permission? Will we exercise courage, letting go the trapeze bar, flying forward toward a new way of being church? It's funny how this faith journey happens. Often in my own experience, and that of my family, we find our way only after we are willing to let go of our former way. I guess that's what faith is about. Faith is what we do when we let go without yet knowing where we are going. Faith is leaving what we know for the land we-know-not-of. May we be found faith-full. May we be captivated by a yearning for God's wide, boundless ocean.

> "If you want to build a ship, don't summon people to buy wood, prepare tools, distribute jobs, and organize the work, rather teach people the yearning for the wide, boundless ocean."
>
> *Antoine de Saint-Exupery*[1]

The work of the Holy Spirit....
Making these three big moves in and through our faith communities is a calling which some cannot deny. After this, some

will not be content returning to church-as-we-have-known-it, having discovered a yearning for something more. This is where the Holy Spirit meets us - at the edge of our comfort zone, glimpsed in our peripheral vision, calling in the middle of the night, teasing our souls with a still small voice, enticing us into the dark which becomes light after the courageous first step. So what now? Follow the Spirit's call. Trust your faith journey. Move ahead. Give into that longing.

For Longing
Blessed be the longing that brought you here and quickens your soul with wonder.

May you have the courage to listen to the voice of desire
That disturbs you when you have settled for something safe.

May you have the wisdom to enter generously into your own unease
To discover the new direction your longing wants you to take.

May the forms of your belonging – in love, creativity, and friendship –
Be equal to the grandeur and call of your soul.

May the one you long for long for you.

May your dreams gradually reveal the destination of your desire.

May a secret Providence guide your thought and nurture your feeling.

May your mind inhabit your life with the sureness with which your body inhabits the world.

May your heart never be haunted by ghost-structures of old damage.

May you come to accept your longing as divine urgency.

May you know the urgency with which God longs for you.

A Blessing From John O'Donohue[2]

Through the grace, power, and love of Jesus Christ our Lord, may it be so.

EPILOGUE

Your Faith Community's Capacity To Shift

Do you feel like you are living in two worlds when it comes to your church experience? On the one had you are drawn toward the Postmodern expression of church, seeing the hope and opportunity to reform ourselves into invigorated faith communities. The energy and excitement, the new spiritual vistas ahead, draw you forward toward experimentation and adaptation.

On the other hand, your church continues doing what it's done. There are ministries to do, programs to staff, resources to develop and choose, invoices to pay, property to maintain, and salaries to pay. We can't simply quit being church-as-we-have-known-it altogether. The results would be disastrous for the church and for individual disciples.

The result is that we are straddling a ditch, trying not to fall in. To make this even more challenging, the sides of this particular ditch are widening even while we try to keep our balance. The ditch is becoming a culvert; one which is widening all the time, stretching toward canyon status. We are stretched and pulled, trying to keep ourselves upright over this ever-expanding gulf below us. We realize crisis is coming. We aren't Stretch Armstrong, with unlimited ability to expand! If the crisis is not already here, we see it coming soon.

My hope is that this book provides a conceptual framework which makes sense of your current reality. Further, I hope this book provides direction for moving ahead. As you start, I don't suggest you stop everything resembling the Modern Era in your church. Instead, start moving toward these big three moves. As you move ahead, disciples will taste of the Lord and find that the Lord is good. Disciples have to experience something of a new identity and missional engagement in order to give up what they know. As you experiment forward, your faith community will gain momentum until a tipping point is reached. Then there is no turning back. May we join God's movement, becoming disciples who partner together toward the transformation of ourselves and this world.

APPENDIX ONE
MAKING THE SHIFT RESOURCES

Last Spring (2015) I spent a day and a half with a large, insightful church staff, engaging the Shift Learning Experience in a retreat format. Toward the end, their pastor challenged me with the following statement and question: "If we are the only people in our setting trying to make these shifts, it's not going to happen. These moves are too large for the church staff to be the only one's on board. What can you do to help us with that?" My answer was less than helpful...."Uh, I don't know." Fortunately, they responded graciously, dialoguing about what they anticipated they would need to lead these three big moves in their congregation. The following resources are a result of that field work.

Making The Shift Field Guide
Anticipated publication date: January 1, 2016
This Field Guide is designed for launching your Making The Shift process through an intense 9-week comprehensive experience. This is what you will find in this Making The Shift Field Guide:

Part One – Small Group Curriculum. When making large shifts, we need ways to process our thoughts, feelings, and experiences with others. This small group curriculum is designed for groups gathering once each week for 9 weeks, engaging the theme of the week from the Shift material. This Field Guide provides original content (not in the book) for each week, preparing participants to engage one another around these three big moves in their small groups.

Part Two – Daily Devotionals. For quite a while now, we have been using a daily devotional guide in our congregational visioning process (*Forty Days Of Prayer*, Pinnacle Leadership Press). Forty Days is a very simple devotional guide, focusing disciples on the essential purposes of our faith and calling of the Church. I'm frequently amazed at the comments about its usefulness and meaning. This experience indicates that disciples who engage the same devotional experience as others in their faith community, discover positive forward movement. The daily devotionals in this Field Guide equip disciples to collectively engage their faith journey's as they travel through the 9 weeks of Shifting toward three big moves. Each week's devotions follow the weekly theme introduced in worship and studied in the small group gathering.

Part Three – Worship Resources. When faith communities coordinate worship, small groups, and daily devotionals around common weekly themes, they create an opportunity for increased morale and momentum. This Field Guide includes worship themes, scriptures to explore, and liturgical resources, as well as an introduction to each week's Making The Shift theme.

Making The Shift Enrichment Weekend

One of our Making The Shift Presenters will join your faith community for a weekend of learning, inspiration, spiritual renewal, and visioning. Some congregations will use this weekend to launch their Making The Shift Process described in the Field Guide. Others will use this weekend as a stand-alone event. Either way, this Making The Shift Enrichment Weekend includes:

- Making The Shift Presenter joining you on campus Friday Evening through Sunday
- Experiential events for the entire congregation on Friday and Saturday
- A block of time for discussion with the staff and lay leadership team about next steps
- Participation in your worship gathering by your Presenter

Our hope is that this Making The Shift Enrichment Weekend will provide a spiritual renewal and deepening opportunity for faith communities.

Making The Shift Coaching Process

Some faith communities who want to engage these three big moves with intentionality may secure a Making The Shift Coach. When you contact us, we will learn about your context, about your current engagement with the Shift material, and then design a process for moving forward. Your coach forms a one-year agreement, including campus visits, coaching, and consulting focused on implementing the Making The Shift Process. We will describe the movements in this process more precisely when you contact us.

Shift Learning Experience for Clergy and Church Staff

We are glad to provide the Shift Learning Experience for your group of church leaders. We have presented so far in a variety of settings and time frames. You can learn more about some ways others have engaged this learning experience on our website at www.pinnaclelead.com.

Contacting Us:
info@pinnaclelead.com
www.pinnaclelead.com
Facebook: Pinnacle Leadership Associates
803-673-3634

APPENDIX TWO
SHIFTS NOT MAKING THE CUT

There comes a time when writing a book when you just have to cut off the creative process. These three big moves are included because they appear so foundational. More shifts are needed as the Church evolves toward fulfilling its calling in this Postmodern world. We considered including those identified below, but they didn't make the cut.

- Excessively Scheduled to Practicing Sabbath
- Complexity to Simplicity
- Life Dissatisfaction to Holy Contentment

Potential Engagement Activity – What would your faith community identify as further or additional shifts needed in your context? You could design a dialogue based activity, with worship before and after, as a way to explore needed shifts as a faith community.

APPENDIX THREE
SERMON MATERIAL, RESOURCE ARTICLES, BLOG POSTS

Sermon – God Is Always On The Move

The following is a sermon...sort of. Perhaps it's more like sermon material. You will notice the laws of grammar are summarily ignored. I'm hoping this allows what needs to be said to flow more freely. Please use it any way you can, adjusting and adapting it as you see fit. I'm confident you will create even better sermon material and sermons, so please share them with me when you do. Include your biographical and contextual information so that I can give credit to you as I share your contribution.

God is always on the move.
Doing, acting; living in the active tense.
From primeval times onward; hovering over the deep, moving through the darkness.
Then when the time was right - creating, bringing into being, exploding actually – initiating the big bang.
God is always on the move.
And then God breathed into life, through millennia of formation, this creature, this being, called humankind. It could walk upright on two legs. It could make language and connect. It had self-awareness. It could reflect on its own existence.

And God moved with this human creature, this human being, in the cool of the evenings...in pleasant circumstances – God and God's creation walked together, moved together.

Yet the human being moved poorly, chose tragically, creating distance between itself and God.

The human being was moved out of idyllic circumstances to a lesser kind of existence.

And God was there too, moving into this world.

God continued to move, seeking connection and relationship with this human being, for God is always on the move, and we as God's human reflections are on the move also.

We have this internal restlessness that wakes us up and pushes us out the door.

These human creatures then wandered the earth, collecting themselves into small bands, which became villages, and towns, and cities.

Culture developed. People evolved. God and people were on the move.

People's identities sharpened and names were changed.

Abram became Abraham. Sarai became Sarah.

And then, when the time was just right, God made The Big Move. Advent. Incarnation.

God joined the human creatures. God moved out of self into another.

God took on flesh and blood and travelled among us.

Our minds are boggled when trying to understand this God movement. This was God's BIG Move.

As a result, the human creatures gathered around this person – Jesus the Christ.

As a result, this band of disciples took shape. The Church was born.
And it too reflected God – it was on the move.
Jerusalem, Judea, Samaria...spreading across the world.
The diaspora – the dispersion – scattering throughout the Middle East, into Europe, down into Africa, and the movement continued.

Now God is on the move, and God's church is on the move.

Fast forward in time....
Long after Emperor Constantine legitimized Christianity. Long after Constantine invited this wandering church into the seats of power by wedding the church and state.
Fast forward to just after WWII – God's people, the Church as we know it...the church on the move, found unusually favorable conditions in Europe and here in North America.
Many factors came together to allow this church to proliferate and flourish – culture, timing, openness, economics, the zeitgeist of the times – all these came together and Christians flourished – And settled down.

No longer did they wander; no longer did they live out a nomadic existence.
No longer did they resonate with this God who is on the move.
No longer were they freed slaves moving through the wilderness.
Now they were accepted, legitimized, recognized.
Now they were insiders, no longer outliers.
Being a part of their group became respected – actually becoming nearly necessary to conduct local business or to run for local office.
And these human creatures, these bands of Christ followers, sat down.

This new place of cultural privilege felt so good.

After being in the wilderness for so long, after wandering through the hot desert sands, after always being suspected of something, after living on the defensive....it felt so good to be cultural insiders.

Now we were "legit."

And we sat, and rested from all our labors, from all our wandering.

And, over time, we forgot. We forgot movement. We forgot the fast flow of fit bodies cutting through the wind...on the move.

But God did not forget.

God is always on the move. God is always on mission. God is seeking and saving and reaching. God is on mission in this world.

And then everything changed.

Another 500 year cycle rolled around.

Favorable sociological and cultural conditions shifted to less favorable conditions.

These Christ followers, these culturally appropriate Christian churches...fell out of favor with their context. Constantine's work unraveled. The fabric of society which gave privilege for these wonderful, comfortable years....this soft quilt of comfort...turned to sandpaper, rubbing the Christian church raw.

Many who were taught a culturally enhanced version of this Christian faith were discouraged.

They despaired and left.

They recognized that culture was the driving force in this church and when culture no longer supported or inhabited this church, their drive and energy were gone.

They recognized that the church knows how to sit – but has forgotten how to move.

This brings us to the primary and pivotal Question of the 21st Century:
"Can God's people remember how to move, how to travel, how to shift and adapt and morph?"

Conclusion – Contextualize to your setting

Article – Warning

The teachings of Jesus are so counter-cultural that I wish Bible publishers would include a warning on the cover. Seeing warning disclaimer statements on devices or in service agreements is not unusual. Perhaps the Bible needs something like this:

Disclaimer Statement:

"The writers and printers of this book take no responsibility for the actions of readers after exposure to the images, concepts, people, and teachings contained herein. All claims due to discomfort and lifestyle disruption will be denied, while all stories of abundant life, deeper meaning, and wild abandon with grace will be celebrated. No discounts or special offers apply – all readers are equally in danger. Reader discretion is advised. Proceed at your own risk."

"Do not look for shortcuts to God. The market is flooded with surefire, easygoing formulas for a successful life that can be practiced in your spare time. Do not fall for that stuff, even though crowds of people do. The way to life – to God! – is vigorous and requires total attention."

Jesus, recorded in Matthew 7:13-14, The Message

I did a dangerous thing again. Ever have one of those things that you know will disturb you and yet you can't look away, or put it down, or ignore it? It's like a scary movie that you just want to walk away from, yet you are hooked. You have to see what happens. Well, that's what happens with this one particular book – the Holy Bible.

I mistakenly picked it up recently, forgetting the warning in small print above, and skimmed over the gospels. I was not at work, so my professionalism was lowered, making me more personally vulnerable to shots from those pages.

The pictures painted of Jesus were the most disturbing. First, he didn't seem to understand the systemic economic and social dynamics that imprisoned people in dire circumstances. He spent much of his waking time, going about, doing good with individuals. Healing, feeding, forgiving, accepting, etc. He looked out over Jerusalem, with a tear running down, and compared himself to a mother hen (lack of dignity). Jesus seemed to think that raising individuals up out of their mess was a worthy use of his time.

Another picture painted therein of Jesus disturbs me. He was highly confrontational with religious people, actually blaming them for systemic and social dynamics that imprison others in dire circumstances. He did not attack the occupying political entity (Rome), but focused his challenge on the oppressive religious system that did not address real life human concerns and conditions. He challenged their personal actions, structures, and religious culture. Didn't he know they were good people, simply trying to do what God wants?

And then, to cap it all off, Jesus is so radically generous with grace. The people he forgives aren't even clear on who he is. They don't have a correct understanding or solid belief before he forgives them. They are not very deserving of grace. In addition, Jesus acts like he could never give all the grace he has away! He doesn't ration it or only give it when conditions are just right. Jesus lives large.

What's this book rated? Where are the disclaimers? People could get into trouble reading this kind of literature. Our world would go nuts if people really lived this way. I'm afraid to pick the thing up again. I think I'll wait until I have others with me to help cushion the blows. You be careful too with that book.

Blog Post – Just Me And Jesus Will Do Fine
"When we are pursuing being disciples of Jesus Christ, we realize we need the church less."
I hope my mouth didn't drop open when he made this statement. The lay leadership team of this healthy church was gathered for their annual retreat. They asked me to guide their experience using the Shift Learning Experience. I was describing the move from member identity to disciple identity. This gentleman seemed to be tracking really well; asking insightful questions and vigorously engaging the learning. But when he made this remark, everyone stopped and stared.

"Tell more about what you are thinking." That's the best I could respond, given my shock about his statement. He went on to describe the process of becoming a disciple more fully as a very privatized and individual activity. He talked about a system of spiritual disciplines one would engage on a daily basis (yes, that's one aspect of it) and how one would go deeper in one's faith journey.

Afterwards, it was clear to me that this gentleman represents many Christ-followers. Many see the process of being formed more fully as disciples as a very personal, private, and individualistic activity. This is something one does behind closed doors, in one's private prayer closet, so to speak. Given this view, one needs the programs and services of the church less and less.

Two insights rise to the surface after reflecting on this experience.

First, I'm reminded that the culture of our context (USA) significantly influences our faith. Here in America we value individuality. Here we believe individuals can pull themselves up by their boot straps. Here we promote John Wayne types as heroes. Would John Wayne ever need a community, a team, to accomplish his mission? No, he goes it alone. "Hyper-Individualism" is not too strong a phrase to describe our cultural context, which then influences our faith.

Second, I'm afraid we church leaders have taught, or at least insinuated, that following Jesus is a very individualistic activity. Protestant evangelical churches have (and some still do) emphasized a VERY personal relationship with Jesus. When we stay with this thought, the VERY part becomes formative. Since we understand the heart of our faith to be about a VERY personal relationship with Jesus, then gathering with other disciples for mutual support, growth, and sharing becomes less important. The gentleman in the retreat simply verbalized succinctly what many Christ-followers believe. Just me and Jesus will do fine.

The irony in this is striking. When we actually try living as disciples of Jesus Christ, we find that we need the church (invigorated community gathered around the Risen Christ) so much more than before. As I seek to LIVE as a disciple, I'm completely sure that I cannot live that way by myself. I've tried it, and failed. Sure I can maintain systematic devotional life on my own. But implementation – actually living the gospel – that's another story. Loving people when I have a schedule to keep, giving away things rather than getting more things, forgiving people who really hurt me…I have to have a community of disciples with whom to ride that river. I can't sustain it on my own. The challenge is too significant.

It turns out that just me and Jesus won't do. Instead Jesus provided for us a community of faith with whom to share the journey. Thanks be to God.

Mark posts blogs two places.

1. Writing about church, leadership, and change….Pinnacle Leadership Associates website, Blog. See www.pinnaclelead.com
2. Writing about many other subjects but not excluding those above….See Mark's personal blog at https://marktidsworth.wordpress.com. You will find this particular blog post at https://marktidsworth.wordpress.com/2015/03/26/just-me-and-jesus-will-do-fine/

Article - How Your Church Can Escape the Happiness Trap
How do you evaluate church? How do you decide if your congregation is doing well?

While many factors influence how a person answers these questions, a popular measure is the "happiness factor." Essentially, members ask themselves how happy or content the majority of members are with the church. If most are, this means the church is doing well. This is a major dynamic flowing through church life in 2013. Add to this contentment tendency the Postmodern influences of our society, and we find ourselves in whitewater times. Some congregations are learning to swim in these strong currents while others are stuck in the happiness trap. In such times, how do congregational leaders, clergy and laity help congregations find their swimming strokes?

Gil Rendle writes a pithy article in an Alban Institute book on congregational happiness, encouraging congregations to consider their core values by asking important questions. Are we about keeping as many people as possible happy? Or are we about something larger and more significant?

My experience with congregations is that most find themselves on a continuum somewhere between these questions. Pastors, church staff and lay leadership teams play out their ministries on the same continuum. How happy or content does this group need to be in order to risk missional ministry? How much security and comfort are needed in this congregation in order to embrace missional change?

These questions reflect the challenge of congregational leaders who seek "to comfort the afflicted, and to afflict the comfortable," as a country preacher once said. Ideally, our hope as Christian people who are heavily invested in Christian faith communities is that we can choose higher purposes.

In "The Illusion of Congregational Happiness," Rendle encourages congregations to refocus priorities onto mission and calling by "learning to make decisions based on their understanding of the congregation's call to ministry or its core purpose, rather than according to an individual's or group's preferences." The false god of happiness needs to go. When congregational happiness is enshrined, God's Holy Spirit is constrained, change is minimized or eliminated, and leadership energy is consumed internally rather than in external ministry. Our world needs more from the church than a lazy float trip. One way to refocus on mission rather than happiness is by paying attention to our questions.

Contentment and happiness questions are:
- Who wants what?
- How do we satisfy (a person or a group)?
- What should we do about (a problem or complaint)?

Purposeful, identity and missional questions are:
- Who are we and who are we called to be?
- What are we called to do in this chapter of our congregational history?
- What are the goals and/or objectives that we set out to accomplish in our ministry?
- What are the appropriate strategies for our ministry, and how will we measure its attainment?

When clergy and laity ask this second set of questions and lead with purpose, the congregation finds an opportunity to define itself by considering whether they are more concerned with contentment or with missional ministry. I am hoping Christian churches will rise up by defining themselves in terms of faithfulness to God's calling because we are about so much more than contentment.

I am hoping we can delay gratification now, serve strong and faithfully, and find contentment in a ministry well done with a world more aware of God's love.

Happiness or faithfulness? May God strengthen Christian faith communities with resolve to swim well.

Ethicsdaily.com picks up many of Mark's articles and blog posts. You can type in Mark's name on their website, finding many article resources. Most of these are on the Pinnacle blog, yet are a bit more difficult to find.

APPENDIX FOUR
MARKS OF A NEW MONASTICISM

"Marks Of A New Monasticism," is a list of 12 descriptors agreed on by a gathering of participants in new monastic-like communities in Durham, NC. They are found in *The Irresistible Revolution* by Shane Claiborne and *New Monasticism* by Jonathan Wilson-Hartgrove (See notes on Chapter 6 for biographical reference).

1. Relocation to the abandoned places of empire.
2. Sharing economic resources with fellow community members and the needy among us.
3. Hospitality to the stranger.
4. Lament for racial divisions within the church and our communities, combined with the active pursuit of a just reconciliation.
5. Humble submission to Christ's body, the church.
6. Intentional formation in the way of Christ and the rule of the community, along the lines of the old novitiate.
7. Nurturing common life among members of an intentional community.
8. Support for celibate singles alongside monogamous married couples and their children.

9. Geographical proximity to community members who share a common rule of life.

10. Care for the plot of God's earth given to us, along with support of our local economies.

11. Peacemaking in the midst of violence, and conflict resolution within communities along the lines of Matthew 18:15-20.

12. Commitment to a disciplined contemplative life.

NOTES

Chapter One – The River In Which We Swim

1. As this book is going to print, word of Phyllis Tickle's death is reaching us. What a good and inspiring contribution she made to this world, and especially to the Christian movement. We are better because of her. May we live better, more like disciples of Jesus Christ, in our Postmodern context because of her inspiring life. Phyllis Tickle, *The Great Emergence: How Christianity Is Changing And Why* (Grand Rapids, MI: Baker Publishing, 2008), Chapter 1.

Chapter Two – When The Current Changes Direction

1. Shawn Achor has gathered insights from Positive Psychology focused on that which leads to a fulfilling and happy life. Though I don't agree with everything Achor suggests, he does base his insights on thorough research. Learned helplessness is a condition we would want to avoid, so learning to understand and identify it is helpful for congregational leaders. Shawn Achor, *The Happiness Advantage* (New York, Crown Business, a division of

Random House, Inc., 2010). Sections on learned helplessness are pp.115-17, 131.

2. Alan J. Roxburgh and M. Scott Boren, *Introducing The Missional Church: What It Is, Why It Matters, How To Become One* (Grand Rapids, MI, Baker Books, 2009).

Chapter Four - The Demise of Member Identity

1. Brian McLaren, *A New Kind Of Christianity*, (New York: Harper Collins Publishers, 2010), pp. 28-9.

2. Mark Tidsworth and Ircel Harrison, *Disciple Development Coaching* (Atlanta: Nurturingfaith, Inc., 2013), pp.105-6.

Chapter Five - The Rise of Disciple Identity

1. Stanley Hauerwas and William H. Willimon, *Resident Aliens: Life in the Christian Colony* (Nashville: Abingdon, 1989). Quoted by Darrell Guder, *Missional Church: A Vision For The Sending Of The Church In North America* (Grand Rapids, MI: Wm. B. Eerdmans Pub., 1998), p. 78.

2. Charles M. Sheldon, *In His Steps.* There are so many reprints of this book. I searched many of them, looking for the first publication date. Finally I turned to Wikipedia (for better or worse), which says 1896. Even with its outdated language, I recommend this book to you.

3. Robin R. Meyers, *Saving Jesus From The Church* (New York: Harper Collins Publishers, 2009), p.145.

Chapter Six – The Disciple Development Movement

1. Marjorie J. Thompson, *Soul Feast: An Invitation To The Christian Spiritual Life* (Louisville, KY: Westminster John Knox Press, 1995), p. 138.

2. Mark Scandrette, *Soul Grafitti* (San Francisco: Josey-Bass, 2007).

3. Shane Claiborne, *The Irresistible Revolution: Living As An Ordinary Radical* (Grand Rapids, MI: Zondervan, 2006), Appendix Two, pp.363-4. See Appendix Four in this book for the list.

4. Jonathan Wilson-Hartgrove, *New Monasticism: What It Has To Say To Today's Church* (Grand Rapids, MI: Brazos Press, Baker Publishing Group, 2008).

5. Michael W. Foss, *Power Surge: Six Marks Of Discipleship For A Changing World* (Minneapolis: Augsburg Fortress Publishers, 2000).

Chapter Eight – The Demise Of The Attractional Church

1. Alan J. Roxburgh and M. Scott Boren, *Introducing The Missional Church: What It Is, Why It Matters, How To Become One* (Grand Rapids, MI, Baker Books, 2009). Introduction.

2. Ibid., p.19.

3. Ibid., p.18.

Chapter Nine – The Rise Of The Missional Church

1. Darrell Guder, ed., *Missional Church: A Vision For The Sending Of The Church In North America* (Grand Rapids, MI: Wm. B. Eerdmans Pub., 1998), p. 4.

2. David Bosch, *Transforming Mission: Paradigm Shifts in Theology of Mission* (Maryknoll, NY: Orbis, 1991), p.390.

3. Guder, p.5.

4. Guder, p.7

5. Guder, p.6

6. Quoted by Alan Roxburgh and Scott Boren, *Introducing The Missional Church: What It Is, Why It Matters, How To Become One* (Grand Rapids, MI, Baker Books, 2009). P.20.

7. Dan Kimball, *The Emerging Church* (Grand Rapids, MI: Zondervan, 2003) p79-80.
8. George Hunsberger, *Missional Church*, p.77.
9. Peter Senge, *The Fifth Discipline, The Art And Practice Of The Learning Organization* (New York: Currency Doubleday, 1990).

Chapter Ten – Making The Shift Toward Missional

1. David Bosch, *Believing In The Future: Toward a Missiology of Western Culture* (Valley Forge, PA: Trinity Press, 1995) p. 33.
2. Michael Frost, *The Road to Missional: Journey To the Center of the Church* (Grand Rapids, MI, Baker Books, 2011) p.24.
3. Ibid., p.24.
4. Roxburgh and Boren, *Introducing The Missional Church*, p.72. Also -Leslie Newbigin, *"Christ And The Cultures,"* Scottish Journal of Theology, 31(1978): 1-22.
5. Brian McLaren, *We Make The Road By Walking* (New York: Jericho Books, Hachette Book Group, 2014)
6. Hans Kung, *The Church As The People of God* (Garden City, NY: Image Books, 1967), pp.59-65.

Section Four – Consumer Culture To Sacred Partnering

1. Meyers, *Saving Jesus From The Church*, p. 160

Chapter Eleven – The Demise of Consumer Church Culture

1. Guder, editor, *Missional Church, A Vision For the Sending Of The Church In North America*, p. 85.
2. Walter Brueggeman, *The Prophetic Imagination* (Minneapolis: Augsburg Fortress, 2001), p.1.

3. Michael Frost, *The Road To Missional: Journey To The Center Of The Church* (Grand Rapids, MI: Baker Publishing Company, 2011), p. 76.

4. C. Christopher Smith and John Pattison, *Slow Church: Cultivating Community In The Patient Way of Jesus* (Downers Grove, IL: InterVarsity Press, 2014).

5. Frost, *The Road To Missional: Journey To The Center Of The Church*, p.69.

Chapter Twelve – The Rise Of Sacred Partnering

1. "America's Changing Religious Landscape."(May 12, 2015, www.pewresearch.org).

2. Meyers, *Saving Jesus From The Church*, p.158.

3. Ronald Heifetz, Alexander Grashow, Marty Linsky, *The Practice Of Adaptive Leadership* (Boston: Harvard Business School Publishing, 2009).

4. Phillip Yancey, *What's So Amazing About Grace?* (Grand Rapids, MI: Zondervan, 1997).

5. Matthew 6:10, *Holy Bible* (NRSV), 70 CE.

6. Guder, ed., *Missional Church, A Vision For the Sending Of The Church In North America*, p.108.

7. Ibid., p.109.

8. Meyers, *Saving Jesus From The Church*, p.159.

Chapter Thirteen – Making The Shift Toward Sacred Partnering

1. To learn more about the research, see Robert Rosenthal's study with teachers and students. A brief summary is found in Psychology Today, Ronald E. Riggio, April 18, 2009.

2. Frost, *The Road to Missional: Journey To the Center of the Church*, p.21

3.

1. Quoted by Alan Hirsch, *The Forgotten Ways: Reactivating The Missional Church* (Grand Rapids, MI: Baker Publishing Group, 2006), p. 27. I can't quit quoting this statement. Ever since seeing it in 2006, I can't lay it down. It seems to capture the zeitgeist of our times...these are days when creativity, adaptation, courage, boldness are needed by God's Church. The kinds of people who exercise these qualities are those captured by the longing for the wide, boundless ocean. The Holy Spirit inspires this kind of living. May these kinds of people find their voices, helping the rest of us follow the Spirit's lead into the next expression of God's good Church.

2. John O'Donohue, *To Bless The Space Between Us: A Book of Blessings* (New York: Doubleday, Random House, Inc., 2008), pp.35-6. Pinnacle colleague and friend Rev. Dr. Alan Arnold introduced me and our team to this book of blessings during the devotional in a team meeting. Alan is a deep thinking, but even more, a deep "faith-er." This book of blessings now provides me a go to resource when the time for blessing comes near. Thanks to A.A. for uncovering this pearl.

Made in the USA
San Bernardino, CA
30 September 2016